"Senator Kirsten Gillibrand's story will prove instructive to anyone who wishes to find her true north, understand power dynamics, and confront entrenched interests when justice is not served. *Off the Sidelines* is required reading for all women who want to change the world and recognize that to do so they must better understand political realities."

—PIPER KERMAN, author of
Orange Is the New Black

"Reading Kirsten's book makes me so proud—as a woman, as an American, and as her friend. She is a beautiful example of what we can become when we are true to ourselves and brave enough to let our voices be heard. This book is intimately honest and deeply insightful. It should be on every girl's and every woman's reading list, and every boy's and man's, too."

—CONNIE BRITTON

"Kirsten Gillibrand is one of the most forward-focused leaders we have working on our behalf, and *Off the Sidelines* is an excellent example of inspiring women to make their voices heard."

—BILLIE JEAN KING

"A must-read for every woman looking to effect change. Gillibrand's secrets to speaking up—whether you're striving for political office, aiming for the boardroom, or simply trying to improve your kid's school—are powerful lessons for women looking to make a difference. After all, if you've worked hard enough to gain a seat at the table but you say nothing, that's a lost opportunity."

—URSULA BURNS, chairman and CEO,
Xerox Corporation

"Senator Gillibrand is a vibrant role model for her generation and makes a strong and very personal case for why we should all care about our government. Her trademark honesty and humor speak loudly to why we need women in the game."

—GERALDINE LAYBOURNE, founder,
Oxygen Media and Kandu

OFF THE SIDELINES

OFF THE SIDELINES

Raise Your Voice, Change the World

Kirsten Gillibrand

WITH ELIZABETH WEIL

Foreword by Hillary Rodham Clinton

BALLANTINE BOOKS

NEW YORK

Published in the United States by Ballantine Books, an imprint of Random House, a division of Random House LLC, a Penguin Random House Company, New York.

BALLANTINE and the HOUSE colophon are registered trademarks of Random House LLC.

LIBRARY OF CONGRESS CATALOGING-IN-PUBLICATION DATA
Gillibrand, Kirsten.
Off the sidelines: raise your voice, change the world / Kirsten Gillibrand with Elizabeth Weil.
pages cm
ISBN 978-0-8041-7907-2
eBook ISBN 978-0-8041-7908-9
1. Gillibrand, Kirsten. 2. Gillibrand, Kirsten—Philosophy. 3. Women legislators—United States—Biography. 4. Legislators—United States—Biography. 5. United States. Congress. Senate—Biography. 6. Women—Political activity—United States. 7. United States—Politics and government—1989– I. Weil, Elizabeth. II. Title.
E901.1.G55A3 2014
328.73'092—dc23   2014024020
[B]

Printed in the United States of America on acid-free paper

www.ballantinebooks.com

2 4 6 8 9 7 5 3

Book design by Dana Leigh Blanchette

For Grandma

FOREWORD

Hillary Rodham Clinton

The first time I shook Kirsten Gillibrand's hand, she looked me square in the eyes and said, "How can I help?" I was running for Senate in New York and Kirsten wanted to do everything she could for the campaign. But there was more to it than that. Kirsten has built her whole life around the question "How can I help?" Wherever there's a problem to solve, a wrong to right, or a person in need, Kirsten rolls up her sleeves and gets to work. Staying on the sidelines just isn't in her DNA. That's been the story of her entire career—as a lawyer, then as a member of the U.S. House of Representatives, and now as a U.S. senator—and it's the story of this book.

Off the Sidelines is a memoir of a life shaped by a deep commitment to family, public service, and hard work—and a story that is far from finished. I hope it will serve as an inspiration to others, especially young women, and encourage them to follow Kirsten's example. The health of our democracy depends on women as well as men stepping off the sidelines to participate—to vote, debate, organize, run for office, and lead.

Kirsten wasn't born a senator, but service is in her blood. Her story starts with another indomitable woman: her grandmother Polly Noonan. At a time when few women were involved in politics, Polly was a force. She was a fixture in Albany and a role model for Kirsten. On weekends, Kirsten stuffed envelopes and slapped bumper stickers on cars, getting her first taste of political participation. Kirsten's mom, Polly Rutnik, was a trailblazer, too—a lawyer, one of the first working moms in the neighborhood. You can see the influence of these women throughout Kirsten's life. Just as Polly often made dinner while balancing a phone on her shoulder, conferring with clients, it's not unusual to find Kirsten on the Senate floor, casting a vote, with one eye on her small sons, waiting for their mom in the hallway just outside. And this is one of the lessons found in *Off the Sidelines* that resonate far beyond Washington. Women across our country work hard every day to juggle the demands of work and family. Sometimes it can seem as if we have to give up one dream in order to pursue another. But Kirsten shows us how much is possible. Women can lift up themselves, their communities—even entire countries. All they need is a fair shot and the chance to participate.

When I accepted President Barack Obama's offer to serve as secretary of state, I wanted someone strong and caring to fill my seat in the Senate. From 9/11 to the financial crash, it had been a rough eight years for New Yorkers. They had taken a chance on me back in 2000, and now they needed an effective and committed advocate in Washington.

Kirsten was a great choice. As a congresswoman, she was a champion for families in her upstate New York district and a creative problem solver willing to reach across the aisle to get the job done for her constituents. And she was a leader on transparency, putting out a weekly "Sunlight Report" detailing exactly how she spent her time. *The New York Times* called it "a quiet touch of revolution." She was just what the Senate needed. A few days before she was sworn in, Kirsten and I sat down for lunch with Governor David Paterson and Senator Chuck Schumer. She told us, "I'm going to hit the ground running." And boy, did she. Practically overnight, Kirsten went from a junior congresswoman to a prominent and powerful senator.

I was particularly pleased that she continued the fight for one of my most deeply held personal priorities: standing up for 9/11 first responders and others who had suffered lasting health effects from their service around Ground Zero. And that wasn't all. No one has been a stronger champion than Kirsten for victims of sexual assault within our military—an issue that's too often been put on the backburner or put off altogether. And she's stayed true to her roots, continuing to advocate for upstate New York and working to create jobs and opportunities across the state. She's even co-captain of the Congressional softball team!

Above all, Kirsten gets results. She has no time for the dysfunction and gridlock that hamstring Washington. We need more leaders like Kirsten, willing to choose common ground over scorched earth.

Like most women who have run for office, Kirsten's faced her share of challenges. Instead of letting those obstacles stand in her way, she's made it a personal mission to help the women coming up behind her. She was just the sixth woman to give birth while in Congress—showing everyone once again that it's possible to be a great mom and a dedicated public servant. In fact, being a mom can make you an even better public servant.

For Kirsten, public service isn't a job. It's a calling. She sees people suffering, or being mistreated—people who aren't getting the shot they deserve, who have the talent and the work ethic but not the opportunity—and she asks the same question I first heard all those years ago. "How can I help?" It's who she is. It's how she's made. And it's what makes her a great senator, and a great friend.

CONTENTS

INTRODUCTION

If I had a daughter, I would tell her certain things. I would tell her that it's great to be smart, really smart—that being smart makes you strong. I would tell her that emotions are powerful, so don't be afraid to show them. I would tell her that some people may judge you on how you look or what you wear—that's just how it is—but you should keep your focus on what you say and do. I would tell her that she may see the world differently from boys, and that difference is essential and good.

These are not the lessons I feel I need to give my sons. They already believe that they are innately strong and powerful and that others will respect their worldview. This hit me when my younger boy, Henry, was two and a half years old, and my husband, Jonathan, took him and Theo, his older brother, then age seven, to Theodore Roosevelt Island to explore. Roosevelt Island is fantastic: right in the middle of the Potomac River and filled with woodpeckers, frogs, marshes, trails, and a seventeen-foot statue of Roosevelt himself, in shining bronze and larger than life. Along one of the paths, the kids came to a hill. Jonathan, sensing a slowdown and not wanting to carry Henry, said enthusiastically, "Come on, boys!"

Henry didn't miss a beat. He just nodded his little chin in agreement and said, "We can do it because we're men!"

Now, I love my sons, and I love Henry's confidence. I want him to think that the world is his. But how the hell did he come to believe, at the tender age of two, that he could do anything because he is a (very little) man? I did not teach him this. In our family, capability has nothing to do with gender. I'm one of only twenty female senators, so I have about as atypical a job as you can find for a woman in the United States. More to the point, how many girls in his preschool class, when faced with some hill to climb, would say brightly, "We can do it because we're women!"?

I can tell you how many: zero. Well, maybe one, Irina—more on her later. That's why I'm writing this book. I want women and girls to believe in themselves just as much as men and boys do. I want them to trust their own power and values and say, "We can do it because we're women!"—not just for their own sense of self, but for all of us. Girls' voices matter. Women's voices matter. From Congress to board meetings to PTAs, our country needs more women to share their thoughts and take a place at the decision-making table.

This is not a new idea. During World War II, Rosie the Riveter called on women to enter the workforce and fill the jobs vacated by enlisted men. The Rosie the Riveter advertising campaign had a simple slogan: *We can do it!* And she told women two things: One, we need you, and, two, you can make the difference. My great-grandmother Mimi and my grandmother's sister, my great-aunt Betty, both saw Rosie on posters, pulled off their aprons, and headed to work at an arsenal in Watervliet, New York, assembling ammunition for large weapons. Throughout my childhood, lamps made out of shell casings from that arsenal lit my great-grandmother's living room. Rosie the Riveter was direct, unconventional, and extremely effective. By the end of the war, six million women, including my great-grandmother and her daughters, worked outside the home. Their generation forever changed the American economy and women's role in it.

We need a Rosie the Riveter for this generation—not to draw women into professional life, because they are already there, but to elevate women's voices in the public sphere and bring women more fully into making the decisions that shape our country.

I first realized this as an eager twenty-eight-year-old who looked up from her law firm work long enough to notice that First Lady Hillary Rodham Clinton was speaking to the world from a stage in Beijing. She was at the United Nations World Conference on Women, and she was delivering to the whole planet a very simple, powerful message: Women's rights and human rights are one and the same. I was floored. I'd majored in Asian studies at Dartmouth and studied Mandarin in Beijing. I couldn't believe Hillary was so bold as to make that speech from China, where the women's rights movement was decades behind the one in the United States. I kicked myself for not being there, for not even knowing about the conference. That woke me up to the fact that there was an important global conversation taking place. I cared deeply about it, and I wasn't participating.

What was I waiting for? An invitation? Thanks to my grandmother Polly, who was involved in Albany politics, I grew up steeped in political stories—it was simply background noise in our family. When I was young, maybe six or seven years old, I sat around with my little sister, Erin, and my cousin Mary Anne, and while they announced that they wanted to be an actress and a flight attendant when they grew up, I said I wanted to be a senator (not that I knew what a senator did, exactly, but I knew it sounded accomplished and important). Yet by high school I'd lost my girlhood bravado. I knew by then that my goal sounded presumptuous for a girl, so I switched to saying I wanted to be a lawyer. But when I heard about Hillary's address in Beijing, my unfiltered childhood sense of self came rushing back. I wanted so badly to have been there in Beijing—and that meant I needed to become more involved in politics. I needed to embrace the part of me that I'd been pushing away.

At the time, I was living in a small apartment with my actress younger sister on the Upper East Side of Manhattan, working far too many fifteen-hour days. Outside work, I was volunteering with a few local charities, trying to make a small difference. But politics was something I hadn't touched since I was a kid, helping my grandmother and her friends elect local candidates. So I called a friend's mother, who had worked for Vice President Gore doing children and family policy, for advice about getting involved. I trusted and respected her, so when she recommended joining the newly formed Women's Leadership Forum, a political fundraising group for women who cared about presidential politics, I did.

A few weeks later, I left my law office early one evening and headed over to the River Club, a few blocks from the Queensboro Bridge, to hear the first lady speak. Nervous and excited, in my best blue suit, I stood in the back of the room. I was exhausted from the treadmill of my life, I was by far the youngest of the hundred women in the room, and I didn't know a soul. But Hillary Clinton said something that changed me: "Decisions are being made every day in Washington, and if you are not part of those decisions, you might not like what they decide, and you'll have no one to blame but yourself."

She didn't know me any better than a potted plant. She wasn't even looking in my direction. But inside I felt singled out. I cleared my throat and started sweating, knowing right then that I needed to alter my life. I was on track to make partner at a big corporate law firm, which would mean a healthy paycheck, more than enough to raise a family someday. But there, in that room, for the first time, I was forced to confront that this wasn't what I wanted for myself. I wanted to do work that mattered to me. I wanted to help shape decisions that impacted people in positive ways. I wanted a life in public service. The idea of running for office terrified me, but deep down I knew I had to. The first lady was right: If women in all stages of life don't get involved and fight for what we want, plans will be made that we may not like, and it'll be our own damned fault. I think about this every day. It's true at every level, from the Capitol to your city's town hall to your neighborhood school. We need to participate, and we need to be heard. Our lives, our communities, and our world will be better for it.

It's almost twenty years later, and I'm still fighting for women to be heard. The landscape for women in politics right now is not pretty. As Gloria Steinem said, brilliantly, "The truth will set you free. But first it will piss you off." So here's my blunt truth: I'm angry and I'm depressed, and I'm scared that the women's movement is dead, or at least on life support. Women talk a lot these days about shattering the glass ceiling, but we also need to focus on cleaning the so-called sticky floor, making sure all women have a chance to rise.

Americans need to demand change. Ours is the only nation in the developed world with no paid maternity leave. We have no paid family sick leave. We don't ensure affordable daycare, or provide universal pre-K, or mandate equal pay for equal work. And what do we do when our representatives fail to fight for these things? Nothing. No axes drop. No booms come down. We do not hold our representatives accountable. When politicians fail to serve constituents on Second Amendment rights or farm subsidies, do you think those voters remain quiet? Not a chance. They respond like wrecking balls, the consequences swift, hard, and unforgiving. We have great women's advocacy groups, with great leaders, but we, as women, don't hold politicians accountable. We don't have a functional women's movement. We need to change that, consolidate our power and shape the national debate. We need to be forceful. We need to be heard.

So this is my Rosie the Riveter moment, a plea to you and all women to get more involved. If women were fully represented in national politics, do you think we'd be wasting so much time debating contraception? Of course not. We'd be fixing the economy, addressing national security issues, and improving education. If women were fully represented in politics, sexual assault in the military and on college campuses would happen less and be prosecuted more—we'd have insisted on transparency and accountability long ago. Caregivers would get the support and respect they deserve. Affordable daycare, universal pre-K, paid family medical leave, equal pay, and raising the federal minimum wage would be foregone conclusions. If women were fully represented in politics, our national priorities would expand and solutions would be smarter and more diverse, and we'd have a stronger economy and nation.

So in hopes of pulling some of you off the sidelines and into the action, I'm sharing here my story from the front lines of public service, as well as stories of brave, outspoken women who have inspired me. I'll also share a few lessons I've learned along the way about inner strength, overcoming obstacles, sharing a bathroom with two boys and a husband, and how to find joy and meaning in life. And I'm going to tell you the most important lesson right here: Your voice matters—to all of us. Together, we can create the country we want and deserve. And we can do it because we're women.

OFF THE SIDELINES

Chapter 1

I'm One of Polly's Girls

My mother took her criminal-law exam two days after giving birth to my older brother, Douglas. A year and a half later, she stood for her New York Bar character exam three days before she gave birth to me. I should note that my mother, while having more strength and guts than almost anyone I've ever met, is only five foot two, so her torso did not leave a lot of room for housing or hiding a baby. Alarmed by the sight of a tiny, very pregnant woman in a huge tent dress, the distinguished gentlemen in the New York State Supreme Court chambers lobbed her three softball questions, told her she passed the character review, and waved her out the door.

The year was 1966. Given that she was one of only three women in her law school class, my mother knew she was doing things differently. She believed in her generation's women's rights movement, but that wasn't what motivated her. She built her law practice alongside her family not out of ideology but because she never considered doing otherwise. She wanted a career and she wanted to be a hands-on, present mom, and she made it work.

As a girl, I wanted to be just like my mother: smart, self-sufficient, in control. I worked hard to be her favorite, but still she treated me, my sister, Erin, and my brother all the same. To this day, my mother likes to tell people that I am the way I am because, according to the Chinese zodiac, 1966 was the Year of the Fire Horse, a once-every-sixty-years event. Sagittarius girls born under that sign are said to be incredibly independent-minded, even disruptive. That may be true of me, but of course my mother and I both know that I am who I am because of my family. My mother and my grandmother are two of the fiercest, most capable, bighearted, and original women I know. They created my frame of reference for women and work. And they taught me the bedrock lesson of life: Be exactly yourself.

From the outside, I had a childhood so conventional it was almost boring. Until I was four years old, my family lived in a tiny clapboard brown-and-white house on Putnam Street in Albany. My dad worked his way through law school, part of the time as a French teacher, even though, he now admits with a laugh, he didn't speak very good French. After Erin was born my parents built a split-level ranch that looked exactly like the *Brady Bunch* house: late 1960s modern, big windows, lots of light. It sat on a cul-de-sac, on the same street where my mother's parents, her aunt, and her two brothers lived. The night we moved in, before our furniture arrived, my mother set a small vase of flowers on a cardboard box that served as a bedside table next to my mattress, one of the thousand domestic kindnesses she doled out between hunting the Thanksgiving turkey with a twelve-gauge shotgun and earning a second-degree black belt in karate.

Every weekday morning, from kindergarten through middle school, I pulled on my school uniform: white shirt, navy blue jumper, blue kneesocks, and blue cardigan. My father then drove my sister and me to the all-girls Academy of the Holy Names while my brother took the bus to Saint Gregory's. At the end of the day, my mother would come straight from work, picking us up at the last possible moment. (We all become our mothers, don't we?) Once home, she'd have dinner on the table within thirty minutes. On weekends, I played hide-and-seek and flashlight tag with my brother, sister, and cousins in the overgrown grass between my parents' and grandparents' houses. Summers, we'd rent a house in Point Pleasant, New Jersey, for two weeks with my father's six siblings—a rowdy crew of aunts, uncles, and cousins.

In many ways it was the stereotypical 1970s middle-class existence—cul-de-sac, family dinners. I even loved Catholic school, especially the older nuns. (I'm godmother to eight children today.) But you didn't even need to nick the surface to uncover the extraordinary. My maternal grandmother's mother, Mimi, lived just down the road from us. She'd worked at the Watervliet Arsenal during World War II, helping to manufacture ammunition for giant guns. She was extremely independent and tough. She kicked my great-grandfather, who drank too much, out of the house and chose to raise her children on her own, though she never divorced or stopped loving him, and when he became sick with lung cancer she took him back and cared for him until his death. My maternal grandmother, Dorothea "Polly" McLean, followed her mother's fear-be-damned lead. Polly was a spark plug, just over five feet tall. She was raised in Albany's South End, and she embodied her tough Irish neighborhood's pugilistic motto: *South End against the world!* Polly never backed down from an argument she knew she could win, and that was pretty much all of them. She told dirty jokes to forewarn men who underestimated her because of her size. She could rattle off strings of expletives as long as a string of Christmas tree lights—five, eight, even ten in a row, never the same curse twice.

I must admit, with some regret, that I inherited her facility for colorful language, though I keep it to one or two expletives at a time. Once, when Senator Joe Lieberman, an elegant and religious man, asked me about the status of a bill, I responded with a recitation of political obstacles that apparently included an epithet I'm sure very few, if any, others had ever used in his presence. A few minutes later, a staffer pulled me aside and said, "You just said 'Fuck me' in front of Joe Lieberman!" I hadn't even noticed, and Lieberman hadn't flinched. God bless his polite heart.

My grandmother didn't go to college. Nobody in her family ever had. In 1936, at age twenty, she married Peter Noonan, a devout young man from Watervliet, New York. Two years later, she took a job as a secretary in the New York State Legislature, and that's when her life started leaping to places most women of her generation never imagined. From the 1920s until the 1980s, Albany was an un-rehabilitated Democratic machine town. One mayor held office for over forty years. By the time I entered politics, the city had progressed, but in Polly's day, Chicago had nothing on the capital of New York. Back then, Albany ran on loyalty and favors. You needed a pothole filled, or your uncle needed a job raking leaves because it would just kill his spirit to be out of work? You called somebody who knew somebody—and, before long, the person you called was my grandmother. She loved her city and the people in it. She always insisted that Albany had no political machine. "It's not a machine! It's a well-oiled organization," she'd say. "A machine has no heart."

In Polly's era, secretaries didn't see themselves as having careers, but they did have real power. They typed letters on old Royal Quiet DeLuxe typewriters with actual carbon paper. Often they wrote the letters themselves; sometimes they drafted entire bills. A clear-thinking, well-spoken secretary reflected extremely well on a legislator's entire office, so before too long, human nature prevailed and the men came to depend on the women. This system of the (perhaps great) woman behind the (perhaps not-so-great) man gave the Albany Democratic Party machine a lot of hidden freedoms. Say party bosses wanted to put a handsome but not well-educated or articulate war veteran on the ticket because they knew he could get elected and would vote with the party. No problem, with the right secretary!

Realizing the invaluable role women played in composing correspondence and maintaining relationships—and unable to restrain herself from filling a need—my grandmother took control of the New York State Legislature's secretarial pool, recruiting and vetting capable talent so that when a new state legislator showed up from Long Island, Buffalo, or New York City for the three-month legislative session, she could match him with a secretary who was an expert writer or a gifted smoother of social gaffes, whatever might be the perfect fit. Before long, Polly found herself in the center of the city's political dealings—helping to organize election campaigns and galvanizing volunteers to staff the polls. She became vital to so many parts of government that legislators began requesting that she be in two or three places at once. Polly, who loved being essential and was also very funny, rose to the challenge. She brought the roller skates she wore in her house's basement into the office. Then she laced them and glided up and down the legislature's grand marble halls, much to the amusement of the press.

To the day she died, my grandmother was in the middle of the action. She worked closely with her mentor, Mary Marcy, the founder of the Albany County Democratic Women's Club, and together with other women, they transformed the way local elections ran. Over time, my grandmother took over the organization, and the women who worked with her started calling themselves "Polly's girls" (inspired by a homemade T-shirt one of them made that read: I'M ONE OF POLLY'S GIRLS). The club did much of the city's grassroots campaigning. They hosted rallies, circulated petitions, threw fundraisers, and knocked on doors. When Mario Cuomo first ran for governor of New York in 1982, he asked my grandmother to organize a women's event. There was a blizzard the day of the event, but five hundred women showed up anyway, and they did so because my grandmother galvanized them. She showed the women of Albany their power to set the agenda and the importance of being involved.

I remember joining the assembly line that Polly's girls formed in the campaign headquarters in downtown Albany one August at the beginning of the election season. I must have been about eight. Ten or fifteen ladies in sleeveless blouses and shift dresses gathered around a long table. I sat among them, mesmerized by their jiggling upper arms as they folded flyers, stuffed and addressed envelopes, sealed and stamped the mailers, and placed their finished handiwork in a box.

My grandfather Peter was quiet, gentle, and thoughtful—a perfect complement to Polly's salty gregariousness and warmth. (I have a similar yin-and-yang dynamic in my own marriage.) While my grandmother hurled herself into politics, my grandfather worked at a freight-car-wheel manufacturing plant and then the new local cement plant. Every year, he prepared Thanksgiving dinner, except for the pies (those were my mom's purview). My brother inherited his culinary talent, and he's the best cook in our family now. My grandfather also played the piano beautifully, and I loved taking piano lessons and practicing at his house. He liked to fish and hunt and welcomed the quiet of the woods—qualities he passed on to my mother, if not to me. To this day, she relishes a 4:00 A.M. trek into a marsh, to be ready when the ducks start to fly. Once, on a hunting trip with friends to Newfoundland, she bagged a moose. She brought it home and butchered it in our garage.

Every Sunday, my grandfather did collections at 9:00 A.M. mass at Saint James in Albany, and every night, he knelt beside his bed for his prayers. For a time, my grandmother broke with the Church over the issue of birth control (why shouldn't a woman plan when to have her babies?), but, like me, she never stopped loving the

Catholic community and the people in it. In those years, the early 1950s, the Sisters of Saint Joseph, the order that taught my mother and her brothers and sister at school, had a very austere life. When my grandparents found out the nuns didn't even have a proper table to gather around, they built one for them, sanding and varnishing the wood to a deep glow. My grandmother always felt sorry for the sisters because, back then, they had to wear thick wool habits, even in the summertime, and the convent buildings had no air-conditioning. So every Thursday during the summer, my grandparents gave their house, with its swimming pool in the yard, over to the nuns. My grandfather would set out food, soda, and beer. My grandmother would lay out cigarettes and ashtrays—"just in case," as she said. Then my grandparents would leave, placing sawhorses across the road behind them so no friends or deliverymen could invade the sisters' privacy. Before too long, word got out among the other convents in the area, as more nuns than just those from the Sisters of Saint Joseph were swimming in the Noonans' pool. That was my grandmother. She took care of people.

She welcomed unmarried pregnant girls into her home, never mentioning the houseguests to anybody in town—or even to my mother or her siblings, who would arrive home from school to find a round-bellied stranger on the couch. One priest my grandmother particularly liked, Father Young, ran a rehabilitation program for ex-convicts and recovering drug addicts in Albany's South End. One morning, as a favor to Father Young, my grandmother drove to Mount McGregor Correctional Facility, picked up a newly released inmate, and brought him back to Albany. Later she learned he had been imprisoned for homicide, but not even that fazed her. Her response: "He was such a sweet boy to me!"

As much as she loved politics, Polly's greatest joy was being a grandmother to my siblings, my cousins, and me. She stayed home and looked after us every Friday until we were old enough to go to school. Throughout my childhood, when I had a stomachache, she'd sit by my side and rub my tummy until I fell asleep. She loved taking us canoeing in her pond, which she always kept stocked with fish, or making jams with grandpa and us with raspberries we picked together from her garden. When we were old enough, she recruited us to work on campaigns, clothing us in matching T-shirts at rallies and cutting us loose to bumper-sticker cars.

She didn't do anything halfway. She used to say, "If it's worth doing, it's worth doing right!" Later in her life, she trained as a drug counselor to help Father Young. Once she got into a shoving match with a reporter but remained unapologetic, claiming that she didn't like the reporter's attitude (as if that were a defense). Only five foot one, she loved ladders and she loved to paint—not landscapes or portraits, the *house*. She kept a pet wolf named Tasha that, according to family lore, was a descendant of the one Nikita Khrushchev gave to John F. Kennedy. (This turns out not to be true, as Khrushchev gave Kennedy a mutt whose mother was one of the first dogs sent into space.) She wasn't much of a cook, except for her cheesecake, which was the best in Albany. She gave the recipe to no one, but if you asked how she made it, she'd deliver one to your door.

One of the most unconventional aspects of my grandmother's life was her relationship with Albany's longtime mayor, Erastus Corning. No one in my family talked about it. I didn't even know it was strange until I was an adult. Polly and Corning met when she was twenty-two and he was twenty-eight. He was the state senator in charge of the Scenic Hudson Commission; she was the commission's secretary. The two of them remained close for the rest of their lives. My grandmother attended parties, Elks Lodge dances, and strategy meetings with Corning, who was married. She often joined Corning as a delegate at the Democratic National Convention. Rumors flew, which my mother and her siblings hated, but my grandmother just lived her life, not caring what others thought. Corning's connection to my family was far more meaningful and complex than almost anybody knew. He may well have been in love with my grandmother, but he also loved the whole family. Most evenings, he sat in a reclining chair in my grandparents' living room, drinking Scotch with my grandfather. Most mornings, he'd drop by the house and drive my mother and her siblings to school. Saturdays Corning worked until noon and then often took my mother, her sister, and her brothers fishing. Some winters, Corning spent a week ice fishing with my grandfather and some other friends in a shack in Maine. In the summers, the extended Noonan family would use the Cornings' camp in Maine when he wasn't there.

From my perspective, the mayor was simply part of our family. He appeared at every family birthday party with the most fantastic present. Once he gave me a miniature microscope, which I loved because it wasn't a frilly girl's gift; it was a serious one, a sign that he thought I was smart and capable of becoming a scientist or a doctor. No one had ever given me a present like that before. He must have noticed how much it meant to me, too, because the next year he gave me a piece of amber with an insect trapped inside. I only remember going to Corning's home once. I was about ten years old. I'd heard that Mrs. Corning kept a greenhouse, where she cultivated gorgeous flowers, and that was indeed true. But what I noticed most at his house were his peach trees and how the fruit needed to be picked. We didn't stay long enough to harvest the peaches, but I desperately wanted to volunteer.

My mother, who was named Polly after my grandmother's nickname, learned to be exactly herself from her mother, and in turn I learned from her. She didn't set out to take her law school exams fresh out of the labor-and-delivery ward. The timing just played out that way, and she powered ahead, undeterred. At age thirteen, she fell in love with my father, Doug Rutnik, a scrappy, handsome boy from the outskirts of Albany and the best athlete in town. "That goddamned Doug, he doesn't even say hello . . ." my grandmother would say with great affection when my father entered her house. He always walked straight to the refrigerator and drank all the orange juice. She admired his bravado, his charm, and his good looks. He was good at every sport he ever tried.

It must have taken heaps of confidence in the 1950s for a man to appreciate all my mother had to offer and all she could do. She worked on the school newspaper in high school, and in college she wanted to try sports reporting. But when she tried to gain access to the press box at the hockey rink, she was denied. In the late 1950s and early 1960s, women did not wear pants in public, and the press box was above the stands, with a metal grate for a floor. Only an immodest young lady would walk, in a skirt, over the open grate above the bench, right? That's not how my mother saw it, and she didn't care what others thought. Her behavior caused such a stir that it was covered in *The Boston Globe*.

At my parents' wedding, my mother held a glamelia bouquet made from white gladiolus and wore a Spanish comb in her hair; she was easily the most exotic bride Albany had ever seen. My brother was born in 1965, nine months and eighteen days after the wedding, and my parents celebrated his arrival with a roast beef sandwich. The birth had not been the most elegant affair, so the sandwich was fitting. Most of the medical residents at Saint Elizabeth's Hospital crowded around to watch my mother deliver. Few had seen a woman go through natural childbirth before.

After I was born, my mother managed to fit in both childcare and her law practice by trading off babysitting days with her friend Carol Bartley, who had two girls, Kathleen and Elaine. Mondays and Wednesdays, my mother took both sets of kids. Tuesdays and Thursdays, Carol did. Friday, my grandmother watched us. My mother didn't know anyone else who did this, and she didn't intend to be a flextime trailblazer; it just made sense. She prioritized both work and family; I never imagined I would do otherwise.

I was a slightly straighter arrow than my mother. Okay, I was a massive kiss-ass and lived for positive reinforcement. As a child, I wrote in perfect cursive penmanship, thanks to the nuns. I did all my homework as soon as I got home, and I kept my room clean. I tattled on my brother and older cousins, payback for them not including me in their games. This was probably for the best, as they were far more adventurous than I. They tried to catch frogs and built potato guns. I liked to organize clubs. My first, with the Bartley girls, was called Cricket. I was secretary and kept meticulous notes.

November 14, 1975

Today we went to the Bartleys' and Erin started to cry. Elaine was shouting. . . . It snowed that morning and it was dark so we could not have the meeting in the fort. In the treasury we have one dollar.

Oh, the joys of governance.

My second club was bigger. We had a proper constitution and dues of ten cents per week.

CONSTITUTION

Article I: NAME
This club shall be known as the U.S. TAG TOE* Club.

Article II: PURPOSE
The purpose of this club is for social enjoyment.

Article III: MEMBERSHIP
Membership in this club shall be granted to those in sympathy with its purpose according to the law of unanimous voting by

confidential means of our officially official vote counter who thereby is, Alison (Cara) Collins.

PURPOSES OF HAVING DUES

1. Anniversary (buy ice cream for all club members)
2. Birthday for club members (buy ice cream just for birthday)
3. Activities
4. Club accessories
5. Tooth decaying molecules (candy)

*TAG TOE stands for The Almost Greatest Things on Earth.

In Brownies and Girl Scouts, I had to earn every imaginable badge and sell the most cookies. A measurable goal, a good cause —sign me up! I didn't just sell to my family and my parents' co-workers. I set up a table at the strip mall and walked door-to-door.

On the tennis court, I learned to deal with stress and competition. At home I learned to argue. My father and I constantly debated: the fairness of pillow-fight tactics, whether I was allowed to go to Saratoga for a concert, if my first car—a blue-and-white AMC Pacer that looked like an inverted bathtub—was too embarrassing to drive to school. I didn't back down easily or quietly. I was on a never-ending campaign to shape and reshape arguments, tinkering until I built a logical framework that allowed me to win.

In response, my father took to calling me Foghorn and Loudmouth, the latter of which he later graciously shortened to Mouth. Those fights, and constantly being challenged by him, helped me develop a thick skin. To this day, I don't let in much negativity or allow myself to feel vulnerable often. This frustrates and bewilders others—"What do you mean, that nasty political cartoon didn't make you want to throttle somebody?"—but it's also allowed me to move forward in a political life.

The nickname Loudmouth summed up the dynamic between my father and me: To him, I was too much, too loud. My mother even had my hearing tested, concerned that I spoke at such a crazy volume. It wasn't just my voice. I was determined to be heard. When I fought with my father, I gesticulated with abandon, so consumed with making my point that I often knocked over my milk. Whatever I did—debating, playing piano or tennis, selling Girl Scout cookies—I had to earn a gold star. In just a few minor areas I didn't strive for excellence. As I wrote in a school paper, in which I was supposed to reflect on myself at age eight or ten: "I am sometimes bossy. I try not to be, but 'nobody is perfect' (except perhaps God). I also tease my sister, but I feel this is natural."

My mother saw in me the determination that marked all the women in my family and gave me the freedom to set my course. For high school, she let me choose between attending Albany High, the big public school with excellent AP courses in downtown Albany, and the Emma Willard School, an elite all-girls school, with boarding students from around the world, located fifteen miles from my house, just north in Troy. Attending Emma Willard was an incredible privilege, I now realize. But at the time I chose the school only after a family friend sat me down at the kitchen table to say I should make my decision solely on where I could get the best education and not on the fact that Albany High had boys. She spoke forcefully about the benefits of an all-girls education, the excellence of the teachers, and the exposure I would have to young women from all across the globe. She believed the choice wasn't even close and that I'd be wasting a precious opportunity by passing it up.

At Emma Willard, I met girls from South America, Saudi Arabia, and South Korea and traveled to France, Spain, North Africa, and Russia on school exchange trips each spring. Those experiences were such a gift. As for boys, I was distracted enough just thinking about them. If there was a party where boys would be present, I planned it—I even planned the dances at school. Even so, I never had a boyfriend in high school, and my crushes amounted to nothing more than dates to formals. On weekends I invited home a carload of friends. Two, three, four girls—it didn't matter. My mother was always welcoming; she preferred having us at her house, where she knew what we were doing. Usually we'd just push together the sectional couches and watch old Hitchcock and Grace Kelly movies, admiring the bold female actresses of the past, like Bette Davis in *All About Eve.*

By age fifteen, we had terrible fake IDs. Not that any of us drank—we just wanted to tag along to the Lark Tavern with my older brother, Doug, and his friends. Half my girlfriends had crushes on one of them. But let's be honest: The 1950s film version of romance playing on the VCR at home was far more glamorous than anything going on at the Lark Tavern.

In many ways, my most meaningful relationship through my childhood was with my sister. We had our bumps, to be sure. When Erin was twelve and I was fourteen, she picked up a charming habit of saying "I hate you" to me. The words hurt far more than she realized, and I told her so in what turned out to be one of the most important conversations I've ever had. Apologizing tearfully, Erin confessed that she didn't realize how much she could hurt me and that she'd just been saying "I hate you" because that's what her friends said to *their* sisters. So I spelled out for Erin the kind of relationship that I wanted *us* to have. I wanted us, as sisters, to be best friends, to give each other advice, to share our innermost truths and have each other's backs, to offer each other unconditional love twenty-four hours a day. Erin agreed that this sounded much better than the I-hate-you sister model. We committed to that positive vision, and Erin remains the person I confide in, the one I tell how I'm *really* feeling about things. She can handle me in all circumstances, and I am grateful for that every day.

Meanwhile, my mother kept on being her self-actualized self. For years, along with playing tennis and golf, she hunted and lifted weights. She even went to see Arnold Schwarzenegger when he was still a professional bodybuilder and he came to talk at the Steel Pier, her old weight-lifting gym. She was already the most badass mom anyone could imagine when, one day, she saw a sign for karate classes at the Steuben Athletic Club, the gym near her office. She enrolled and spent the next ten years practicing at the local dojo and making regular visits to practice with a sensei in New York City, happy to pursue a sport that focused on inner strength, not just outer. Still, back at home, she'd take off her white *gi* and bake cookies with my friends and me, all the while emptying the dishwasher and talking on the phone to file the details of an adoption case she was working on. That's her essence: moving quickly and doing three things at once, powerful and fully engaged with her family, law practice, and life. The phone in our kitchen had a very long cord, but we still had to replace it every few years as she was always pulling it off the wall.

My mother later told me she baked cookies with my friends for two reasons. First, so she'd have homemade treats for the packs of teenagers who passed through our home. But second, and more important, to show us that you could be a woman who worked as an attorney and trained in karate and also be an attentive, involved mom. She must have had an impact, because I didn't think twice about becoming a lawyer, and five out of my six closest girlfriends ended up as lawyers, too. She was one of the few mothers who worked, and I am continually thankful for the example she set. She was permissive but careful, trusting but involved. She sewed for us, when we were young, the most beautiful clothing we owned. And all the while, she never wavered in her commitment to live the life she wanted for herself. She never boxed herself in by positioning her own goals at odds with the family.

My father was the one who came to all my soccer and tennis games. He loved to watch me compete. And, whether intentional or not, he did train me well for my job today. My years of sparring with

him have been invaluable in helping me understand my male colleagues. From my father, I learned how to tell when men stop listening and how to read their emotional cues. (Along with fidgeting and
seeming distracted, their answers become monosyllabic and they
tend to agree more.) When my father fell into that mode, I'd say,
"Can we please talk about this later?"

But ultimately, my mother—and my grandmother, too—cut the
tracks on which I've traveled through life. They had more figured
out decades ago than many women of my generation do now. They
realized that they didn't need to view the key pieces of their identi-
ties in either/or terms. Life is complex. You work, have a family,
give to your community, pursue a physical life and your faith—and
you don't compare yourself to other women, because, as everybody
knows, there's no happiness down that route. Some days I reach
7:00 P.M. desperate to crash when one son needs help with fractions
homework, the other one is begging to play Plants vs. Zombies, and
I'm wrung out from colleagues fighting me. I begin to wonder why
I've chosen this crazy life. But it's in those very moments that I try
to channel my mother and grandmother. I know they wouldn't
flinch. They'd just kiss the boys, go to sleep, and try again
tomorrow—and be exactly themselves.

Chapter 2

From A to B, with Detours

If you're like me, you're reading this book because you want to find out how to get to where you want to be in your own life by learning how someone else got where they wanted to be in theirs. I keep stacks of books next to my nightstand by and about female leaders, and always I have one question: "How'd she do it?" Too often I don't find useful answers, and I close the book, annoyed. I wish I could offer you the perfect parable on how to get from A to B. But I can't. So this is my idiosyncratic story of growing up and building the life I wanted, along with a few lessons I hope someone can use.

It starts with a formidable woman: my Dartmouth squash coach, Aggie Kurtz.

Before I met Aggie, I played JV tennis. My coach was an expert tactician, and he upgraded my forehand and my doubles strategy. I could have gone on playing tennis squarely within my comfort zone, had I not met Aggie. Aggie was one of those coaches young athletes dream of having. The kind of person who believes in you, and also sees right through you, and who, without you noticing it, molds you into the person you need to be.

Because not that many people play squash in high school, Aggie pulled together a squad by scouting among the field hockey, tennis, lacrosse, and soccer players for girls who seemed hardworking, coordinated, and fit. Except for one or two players, no one on the team started with any skills. Few of us even knew how to swing the racquet or where the squash courts were. But Aggie, in her tracksuit, with her no-nonsense haircut and kind blue eyes, led us to the courts and taught us the basics: to stay low and lunge for the ball, and to hit the ball hard from high to low, with a chop and a snap, instead of low to high with topspin, as in tennis.

Squash matches consist of nine players from one team playing against nine players from another: the best against the best, the second best against the second best, and so on. After I got the hang of the game, I often played fourth or fifth, where I could hold my own. Then one day Aggie put me at number two, for a match at Yale. I knew this would not go well.

Just driving into New Haven, Connecticut, which was still considered pretty unsafe in the mid-1980s, was a little intimidating for a girl who'd grown up in Albany and always gone to all-girls private schools. But I was with my team in our van, so I told myself it was just another match. My roommate Regina and another friend drove down in their own car to cheer me on. On the way, Aggie consoled me: I'd be fine; it was good experience to play up. But I'm a very controlled person, and the possibility of losing scared me.

Yale's big, cold Payne Whitney Gym did nothing to put me at ease. In the locker room, I changed into my green tennis skirt and a white tennis shirt. I put my hair up in a ponytail, secured it with a white sweatband (yes, it was the eighties), and walked up to the fourth-floor courts.

The first shot of our match tanked my confidence, and nothing buoyed it from there. The difference between my ability and my opponent's was vast, pretty much like sending your local tennis pro onto a court with Serena Williams. My opponent was much stronger and faster than I was. She had better down-the-line shots and a superior serve. With each point, I felt less in command of the sport's basics. Why did I ever think I could do this sport? I could barely reach the ball, and when I did I couldn't hit it with accuracy. No point lasted longer than thirty seconds.

When the first game ended, I was devastated, my self-esteem destroyed. I walked off the court for a water break, and the minute I saw Aggie, I burst into tears.

Between sobs, I managed to say, "I can't keep playing this match. This girl is just destroying me. . . ." I was shaking, on the edge of hyperventilating, and ready to quit.

Aggie just smiled. "Yes, you can," she said. "You can play this match. Do your best with every point. Focus on the game." I nodded. "All I want from you is for you to play your best—nothing more and nothing less. Can you do that?"

I felt like melting into the floor. I said, "Yes."

That was it. I walked back on the court and played out the match, trying to stay mentally and physically focused. I didn't play brilliantly, but I hung in. I was relieved to realize that Aggie didn't expect me to win. I can't say I enjoyed the match, but by the end of it I knew that I would be better off for it—from seeing up close how a faster, stronger opponent played; from having my flaws so glaringly exposed. I never played in the number-two spot again, but I think about that match far more often than the ones that I won. Aggie taught me something important (and that we all seem to need to learn for ourselves): Don't be afraid to fail. Failure is instructive and necessary. Winning is great, but quitting is how you really lose.

I'm amazed at how often my mind drifts back to that match now that I'm in Congress. A strategist or a staffer will say to me, "We can't take on this issue. There's no way we'll win." And I'll remember Aggie. A lot of good intelligence comes from fighting your hardest even if the round ends in defeat. Being willing to risk loss has been a key part of my success in so many important moments of my professional life: my first election campaign, the repeal of Don't Ask, Don't Tell, passing the James Zadroga 9/11 Health and Compensation Act, fighting the entire Department of Defense over sexual assault in the military.

I went to law school at UCLA, which I'd chosen so I could follow my first boyfriend, whom I thought I would marry. He had hoped to do his medical residency in Southern California, where he was from, but matched in Chicago after I accepted my offer from UCLA. We broke up a year later. After law school, I was delivered from my sheltered student existence into life as a young lawyer in New York City working at a big white-shoe law firm called Davis Polk & Wardwell. My goals were earnest and orthodox: I wanted to be taken seriously, to be given a fair shot, and to make partner, though in hindsight I realize I didn't quite know how to achieve that.

I'm a big believer in making your own luck—or, really, putting yourself in the best possible position to take advantage of your circumstances. If something good happens, you need to be ready for it. For this to happen at a law firm (luck at a law firm almost always means making partner) and in many other fields, you need more than a mentor. You need a sponsor. The difference between the two is crucial. Sylvia Ann Hewlett, an economist who studies gender politics, puts it this way: Mentors advise; sponsors act. Mentors give; sponsors invest. Aggie was a mentor: She cared about me, saw my strengths and weaknesses, and helped me become the best version of myself. She gave a lot and received little. Sponsors, on the other hand, expect something back. They invest their clout and political capital in you, and in return they demand that their protégés be loyal and perform. The sponsor relationship is transactional, not emotional. Sponsors succeed when you succeed, and they lose when you lose. They can make a vast difference in a career.

I didn't know any of this when I was at Davis Polk. I was too young and too inexperienced. And I missed a few opportunities because of it.

Which is not to say that I didn't work hard. Boy, did I work hard. I didn't care how many hours I put in or how many weekend or vacation plans I canceled. (I even canceled my first chance to meet my future husband. A friend invited me to join a group of ten planning to attend a black-tie gala together, but I had to work all weekend and couldn't even break away on Saturday night.) I was single, with few responsibilities. Working until 9:00 P.M. or midnight just meant that I'd miss meeting friends or I'd go to bed later.

My focus was on the office, where I was deliberate about how I carried myself, how I did my job, and what I said. I wanted to be seen as an excellent lawyer, not an excellent *woman* lawyer. I wore flats or two-inch heels. My business suits were all black, gray, navy, and brown. (Adventurous for me was a red Talbots jacket, which I wore with a white shirt, navy skirt, and pumps. I had one hot-pink Talbots suit, with faux-pearl buttons, which was mostly for weddings.) From watching the older women at my firm, I gleaned that high heels or body-hugging dresses were not rewarded. One lawyer a few years ahead of me ventured beyond the corporate uniform, and she never made partner or got the respect she deserved. Admittedly, an equally smart, if not smarter, female colleague who dressed head to toe in Brooks Brothers didn't make partner, either. Regardless, I played it safe.

My plan seemed to work, at first. The partners liked me because I was capable, dedicated, and eager. They also knew I'd played tennis at Dartmouth, so they often asked me to replace a missing fourth in a doubles match. I filled in for two different games: one foursome at the River Club, the other at Grand Central Terminal. The matches were aggressive. One of the litigators, Jimmy Benkard, started each game by whispering, "Take no prisoners!" (When he sent a donation for my first campaign, he wrote that one sentence on the card he enclosed. I hung it on my bulletin board and didn't take it down until we won.)

I loved the matches. I played often and grew to know those partners well, but I also felt a little uncomfortable. I worried about coming across as fun-loving and sporty at the expense of serious and smart. Was this a legitimate concern? I had no idea, and at the time I didn't have anyone to ask. I had a few women mentors at the firm, but their advice remained in the realm of office politics and the importance of accepting the tough assignments.

After about a year and a half of playing tennis with the partners, I decided the games could hurt me in the long run, so I informed them that I was focusing on squash and stopped joining their games. I now think that was a mistake. Those matches were a great opportunity to let my bosses know that I was tenacious and fearless, qualities that would serve the firm well. Maybe if those partners saw those traits, one would have sponsored me and taken me under his wing, but, like many twenty-five-year-olds, I didn't place enough importance on personal relationships. I believed my capabilities would just shine through and I'd be successful on my merits alone. It's always more complex than that.

One of the most lasting pieces of advice I got during my Davis Polk years came during a sabbatical I took to work as a law clerk for Judge Roger Miner, on the Second Circuit Court of Appeals. His chambers were in Albany, and my co-clerks and I all had quirky little jobs. In addition to our more serious duties, one of us was the driving clerk, another the library clerk, and I was the soup clerk, which meant I ran the errand of buying the judge his lunch—a cup of soup. I loved delivering it to him in his chambers and having a few minutes to chat about an opinion I was drafting. He took time to help improve my legal writing, but in some ways the most important thing the judge did for me was call me Kirsten. I know that doesn't sound like much, but up until that point in my life—ever since I was a baby and my big brother, Doug, couldn't pronounce my name—everybody called me Tina. Judge Miner would have none of that. Kirsten was my formal name, and he was a formal man, so Kirsten it was.

I assumed I'd go right back to being Tina when I returned to Davis Polk. But shortly after I moved back to New York City, I had dinner at an Italian restaurant with my sister, my father, his girlfriend, and their friend Barbara Jones, who was a judge, too. My parents had separated when I was in college, which came as a surprise to me. Growing up, I always saw them as a perfect couple. They shared a law practice as well as half a dozen hobbies, everything from hunting to golf to gardening. At the time they split I'd had exactly one boyfriend, and the disintegration of their marriage left me so sad, disappointed, and disoriented that for many years my thinking about my parents' relationship was black and white: mom good, dad bad. I didn't know anything yet about marriage and how challenging it can be.

That night at the restaurant, I told Judge Jones about Judge Miner and that I wasn't sure how I'd like to be addressed now.

Judge Jones was very definite, saying, "You know, you really should use Kirsten."

I was surprised she cared.

"Yes," she said firmly. "Tina is too diminutive. You're a big New York City lawyer. You can't possibly go by Tina. Your real name has more gravitas. It's a better name."

Kirsten? It still hardly sounded like myself. But I took her advice. I was already a diligent student of how women are perceived, and I realized that, for better or for worse, something as simple as whether you went by a nickname could impact how seriously you were taken. So from then on I introduced myself as Kirsten. Still, to this day I adore hearing someone shout "Tina!" from across a crowded room. It's a sure sign of family or a very old friend.

Life at Davis Polk was a grind. For nearly five years I traveled what felt like almost every week, spent ten to fifteen hours a day reviewing documents in windowless conference rooms, and drank way too much Diet Pepsi. To alleviate the tedium and stress, my friend Kathy Baird and I ran almost every day we could. (I finished the New York City marathon twice.) For a few years I also lived with Erin, my sister. She was a perfect counterpoint for me, especially at that stage of life. She was a renegade struggling artist, and I was a straight-and-narrow fancy-pants lawyer. She worked as an actress off-off-Broadway and did commercial work whenever she could. I covered the rent, bought groceries, and paid for our weekly sushi dinner dates. On weekends, I sponsored a student in a program dedicated to taking C and D students out of public high schools, mentoring them, and paying their tuition for parochial school. That meant on Saturdays, I'd take the subway uptown, several stops past Harlem, to see Melissa, one of these students. We'd watch a movie or walk around Central Park, and I'd encourage her to stick with math, at which she excelled. After high school she enrolled in New York University, but later dropped out for financial reasons. I wish I hadn't lost touch with her. I think about her often when I'm advocating for affordable college tuition or science and math education for girls.

My own life, while tidy on the surface, was a bit of a mess underneath. Throughout my twenties and early thirties, I was always looking for a guy that I considered a catch. To me, that meant a man who was good-looking, athletic, smart, talented, promising, hard-working, or all of the above. My relationships tended to last four or five years and end in either disappointment or disaster. Some of the men I dated undermined my sense of self-worth, convincing me that I wasn't smart, attractive, or interesting enough. One even became hostile and controlling. I needed to find a way out, which proved harder for me than I expected. I started worrying about myself. Friends and family grew concerned, too.

Breaking my bad relationship patterns became a priority, and somewhat to my surprise, faith helped me a great deal. I started attending a weekly women's Bible study class, and quickly grew to adore it. Once I started thinking more about faith, I began to see how lost I'd been. I needed to find a partner who was loving and kind. A man who would make me happy and would also allow me to thrive. Jonathan came along at the right moment. He's handsome, charming, and sharp-minded, and he also exudes a thoughtful and generous kindness—the whole package. I was intrigued.

After I'd canceled that first date (the gala with a group of ten, including some of Jonathan's friends from Columbia Business School, where he was studying at the time), we finally had a proper one, and it was fantastic: brunch, followed by browsing in Barnes & Noble, then a walk, a trip to midtown to pick up some work (yes, romantic), the evening "singles" mass at church, dinner, and a stroll back home, ten hours after I'd left. I felt so happy and comfortable with Jonathan from that first day. He never made snide remarks. He never insinuated that I wasn't entitled to an opinion. Never said that I wasn't his type, or that I ran funny or that I needed to lose five pounds. It's amazing how many strong, self-empowered women get caught up in bad relationships. I know you all know this, but believe me: You really do want to go for the nice guy, not the hot, flashy, or cool one.

On Sundays, during those years of trying to sort out myself and my love life, I'd go to church. For six years I attended a progressive evangelical church—a bit odd, since I was raised Catholic, but I really liked the preacher. I also taught a Bible study class to ten-year-olds, and I joined the church community in volunteering to help those most in need, in part through the Little Sister Project, dedicated to assisting women who'd been prostitutes and in jail to integrate back into society. Raising money for the Little Sister Project was my first foray into fundraising, and I honestly enjoyed it. I didn't expect this; all anybody ever says about fundraising is that it's awful. But I was hooked when I realized that the money isn't for you—it's for creating a change that you believe in.

The voice that motivated me to take my life in a new direction came from a woman in a pink suit. On September 5, 1995, Hillary Clinton, then still first lady, spoke at the Fourth World Conference on Women in Beijing, China. At that point, my work at the firm was not capturing my heart, and on that day, Hillary said her line about women's rights being human rights, a line that I've repeated almost once a week for the past ten years. Her words were so simple, brave, and powerful, and when I heard them, something woke up in me. I cared about China. I'd majored in Asian studies and spent a semester there in college, devastated by the poverty and pollution but inspired by the culture and the strength of its people. I even spoke passable Mandarin. With her words, Hillary put me back in touch with my childhood dream. I needed to alter the course of my life and get involved in politics. That was who I was and who I had always wanted to be. It was time to embrace what mattered to me most and overcome my fear that others would disapprove of my ambition or view me as presumptuous or entitled.

My family's political world was all back in Albany, so I called a friend whose mother, Nancy Hoit, was active in politics nationally. When I called Nancy, she couldn't have been nicer. She told me to join the New York City chapter of the Women's Leadership Forum. The organization, in turn, said they'd be just thrilled if I joined. All I needed to do was write a check for $1,000.

My first thought was "That's a lot of money!" (My actual thought might have included some swearing.) I'd never written a check that large except to pay my rent. My salary as a single attorney was much more than I needed, but even so, I got a little anxious filling out the "Pay to the Order of . . ." line and the amount. But I did it. It was the one piece of advice I'd been given about getting involved in politics in New York City, so I took it.

My grandmother Polly had taught me that, in politics, you do what's needed. If a candidate you support needs an envelope stuffed, you stuff an envelope. If that candidate needs a breakfast hosted, you host a breakfast. When you believe in a cause, you aren't picky; you just help. In New York City, I quickly learned that what candidates really needed help with was raising money. So that's where I focused my energy. I liked the challenge—it wasn't unlike selling Girl Scout cookies, piquing my competitive instincts by providing a measurable goal.

My early days working in politics in New York City had none of the gritty charm and romance of a room full of Polly's girls in their sleeveless shirts. But I threw myself into it. The Women's Leadership Forum supports Democratic nominees for president. The women involved knew everything and everybody, or so it seemed to me. From them I learned why supporting candidates directly is crucial. Until that point in my adult life, I had never said, even to myself, "Politics is important to me." Now I did, and it was one of those great young-adult epiphanies, an exhilarating moment of clarity when you stop traipsing down the path you're following and discover the one you really want to be on. I didn't run for Congress for ten more years. But that was the first step in defining where my life would go.

As a direct result of writing that check, I found myself in 1995 listening to the first lady that day when she came to speak at the River Club. As I stood in the back of that ornate room, she said the line that woke me up and that I still repeat: "Decisions are being made every day in Washington, and if you are not part of those decisions, you might not like what they decide, and you'll have no one to blame but yourself."

Those words cut through me. If I went into politics, I risked giving up financial stability, but I knew I couldn't just keep volunteering: I had to figure out how to make public service my job. So I joined every board and political group I could, and I sought out political mentors.

When you want to be taken seriously in politics, you have to prove you can deliver, often financially. But as I soon learned, getting people to write checks to a political organization or candidates isn't nearly as easy as getting them to support, say, the Little Sister Project. Nine out of ten people don't care much about politics, and the contributions aren't tax deductible. I had to beg my Davis Polk friends to come to events, which they usually did just to be nice. (I think a lot of my friends still come to political events only to be kind to me.)

Then, in 2000, Hillary Clinton declared she was running for Senate from New York. I was beyond excited. Here was this incredible woman who had influenced me so much, running to be my senator. I tried to get hired by her campaign office, but I didn't get far. I had no experience, and I wasn't all that well connected yet. The fundraising I'd done and the donations I'd made were very small ball. Jonathan, who by that point was my boyfriend, thought I should step up my contributions. "If you really love politics and want a future in it, then you really need to invest your money, too," he said over dinner one night. I was making close to $200,000 a year, far more than I needed. So he suggested I increase my donation budget from $2,000 to $10,000 a year.

The whole notion made me anxious. These days I'm constantly trying to get women more comfortable with political giving. A lot of women, myself included, give themselves license to spend money in ways that project their values if they are related to their family or their home. But that does not seem to translate to political action or supporting candidates. Men seem more comfortable spending money on a wider scale, often to project their power. We all know the cliché of the man buying the flashy car in the midlife crisis. In my experience, men write big checks to political candidates for similar reasons: to make themselves feel powerful.

So I wrote another $1,000 check to attend a Hillary Clinton fundraiser at the beautiful Upper East Side home of Felice Axelrod, a major Hillary supporter. The apartment was elegant, filled with modern art and beautiful flowers. A new friend, Helen Cook, who'd worked on political campaigns for forty years, had suggested that I arrive early so I'd have a better chance of speaking with Hillary. So I put on my best gray wool suit and arrived at 5:15 P.M. instead of 5:30 P.M., joining a dozen other early birds nearly as enthusiastic and starstruck as myself. With a glass of red wine and an absurdly broad smile, I waited for my chance to talk to Hillary. When I reached her, I started gushing. "I'd love to do anything to help you. Really, I would just love to help in any way I can. It would be my pleasure. I'm so excited about your campaign."

"I'd love that," Hillary said graciously. She clutched my hand for a moment and then we were done, Hillary moving on to the next woman waiting in line. But I clung to our brief encounter. Next morning I called Hillary's campaign headquarters to report to her staff that Hillary had told me, herself, that she would love my help. When this did not translate into anything besides a chance to make phone calls and stuff envelopes, I dipped back into my donation budget and spent another $1,000 to attend another Hillary fundraiser, this one at donor Charles Myers's house in Tuxedo Park, about an hour from New York City.

That time, when I reached the front of the reception line, I said to Hillary, "I followed up with your staff about helping, but they said there was nothing in particular they needed right now, so I'm just volunteering in the headquarters. But, truly, I'd love to help in any way I can. I'll do whatever it takes to get you elected."

Hillary focused for a moment. "I would love you to do one thing," she said. "I would love you to host a fundraiser with young women your age."

"Oh, I can do that!" I said. "I'll get that done!"

Hillary gave me her assistant's card, and the next day, feeling triumphant, I called and announced, "The first lady said she wants me to host a fundraiser with young women my age, and I'm going to do this for her!"

The assistant was patient and passed me on to the fundraiser in charge of events, who was more skeptical. (Staffers often have to undo offers made by their bosses, many of whom want to say yes to everybody and leave no one disappointed.) After a month of me calling and saying, "Hillary actually asked me to do this. I promise you, I'll raise fifty thousand dollars! Look, here's my finance plan for the event!" they finally agreed.

You have never seen someone more fervent about organizing an A+ fundraiser. Hillary had asked me to throw an event for young women, so I was going to throw the best event that anybody had ever attended. I proceeded to enlist seventy co-hosts: all my friends and every young woman I knew with an interest in politics, many of whom I'd met at fundraisers I'd helped organize for other candidates over the past few years. I nailed them down, saying, "This is really important. You have to sell three tickets and buy one yourself." Regular tickets were $250 and VIP tickets were $500, meaning each host was asked to raise $1,000 minimum. I was preposterously meticulous and micromanaged everything. I must have called Hillary's campaign office five times to discuss the invitations alone. Did they agree that I should use blue and yellow, as those were Hillary's favorite colors? I'm sure I drove everyone crazy.

The fundraiser, held in the beautiful and ornate Russian Tea Room, with its rich green walls and gold dining chairs, was my first political success—three hundred women under forty, many rushing to the front of the reception line to ask Hillary passionate questions about education and healthcare. We raised our goal and nearly half as much again. Afterward, Hillary sent me a beautiful signed photo and phoned to thank me for my hard work. We chatted for two minutes. That call meant so much to me.

In the years since then, Hillary has offered me feedback at key times. But before I ran for office, our whole relationship consisted of a series of two-minute conversations. The only exception was a personal call about a year or so after she won her Senate race, to tell me how much she liked my dad. He and Hillary both happened to be at the same small birthday party, and the two of them got to talking and had a blast. My father is a charmer. Men love him; women love him. He's fun and a good sport.

"Oh, I had a lovely time with your father. He was just so funny! We talked all about you," Hillary said on the phone. I started laughing, stunned. My father and I did not always have an easy time. This was the first occasion that Hillary and I had ever talked about anything besides politics, and she'd called to gush about my dad.

Three minutes later, head still spinning, I reached my dad. "Guess who just called me!" I said. He chuckled and said he thought Hillary was delightful. A mutual-admiration society!

Being able to ask Hillary for advice at a few very critical times in my political career has been invaluable. I'm not kidding when I say that, until I reached the Senate, the sum total of time she spent talking to me was less than ninety minutes. But that's all it took for her to help change my life, and I would happily work twice as hard to earn that time again. That is the power of a good mentor. Now when young women interested in politics ask me for my time, I always try to say yes, because Hillary said yes to me.

My Hillary party-planning efforts did not solve my problem of needing to find a way to break into public service. I had already tried and failed to get hired at the U.S. Attorney's Office for both the

Southern and Eastern Districts of New York. I'd also written letters to the Ford Foundation, the Carnegie Corporation, and the Rockefeller Foundation—no response from any of them. My spirits were tanking. I couldn't even get a full-time job on Hillary's campaign.

Feeling discouraged, I went to hear Andrew Cuomo, who was then serving as Secretary of Housing and Urban Development under President Bill Clinton, speak at a Women's Leadership Forum event. He gave a fired-up talk about public service, why it mattered, and how we should all be working to make the world better. To which I responded: "Great." I wanted the life he was pitching, but no one was giving me a chance.

So after the talk I walked up to Andrew, introduced myself, and said, "Mr. Secretary, I loved your speech. I agreed with everything you said. But I have to tell you, it's not so easy. I've been trying to break into a career in public service for a couple of years now, and I cannot get my foot in the door. Not at the U.S. attorney's office, not on Hillary's campaign. I'm hardworking, well educated . . . and I can't break in. It really seems to me that it's an insider's game."

"Well, what do you do?" he asked.

"I'm a lawyer at Davis Polk. I'm an eighth-year associate."

Andrew said, "Would you consider moving to Washington?" (Andrew's a very direct and provocative person.)

"Of course," I said, though in the back of my mind I was thinking that I would never move to Washington, because I loved New York, I had a serious boyfriend, Jonathan, and I was up for partner soon. Sure, I'd been dying to break into public service, but now that it was sounding more real, was I willing to walk away from a great, healthy relationship (a big deal for me), a place I loved, and a comfortable, high-paying job?

Andrew said, "Well, if you're really serious about it, I'll have my chief of staff call you tomorrow and set up an interview for next week."

The next day, a Friday, Andrew's chief of staff called. The following Monday, I flew down to Washington. Andrew interviewed me in his bland government-issue HUD office—navy couches, navy carpet, federal medallions on the walls. We talked for twenty minutes, and then he offered me a job on the spot.

"So, are you going to take the job?" he asked after I'd been sitting in stunned silence for fifteen seconds.

"I just need to think about . . ."

"Oh, you weren't serious."

"I promise I'll let you know tomorrow," I said. "I'm really grateful, I think this is just a wonderful opportunity . . ."

"I'll make you special counsel. I'll pay you the highest salary I can under the federal rules, because I know you're leaving a well-paying job. Will you take it?"

I told Andrew that I really needed just twenty-four hours. Then I flew home to discuss it with Jonathan.

We didn't live together at the time, so I met Jonathan at his fourth-floor walk-up on the Upper West Side (his apartment number was eight, my lucky number).

"What do you think?" I asked after I explained to him what little I knew about Andrew's offer.

Jonathan's response was perfect: "All you've ever wanted to do since I have known you is public service. I'll see you on weekends. Screw Davis Polk."

If I hadn't already fallen in love, I would have right then. Jonathan reassured me that I didn't need to worry about him, even though we'd only been dating a year. So the next day, I spoke with the Davis Polk partner I trusted most and gave the firm just two weeks' notice, which was nearly unheard of. The partner didn't say, "But you can't leave! You're about to make partner!," which is what I hoped to hear. (Not that I would have stayed, but it's always nice to feel wanted.) I put most of my belongings in storage and moved down to Washington, D.C. I knew that if things didn't work out, I could always come back.

But I didn't miss corporate law for a second. I got an apartment just two Metro stops from my office and stayed until 8:00 or 9:00 P.M. each night, never leaving before Andrew did. I loved the work. I was helping labor leaders form job incentive programs for single mothers living in housing authorities. I was also working on financing for basic improvements in inner cities. I officially had the bug for public service; there was no turning back now.

Jonathan came to visit me nearly every weekend, and on the ones he didn't, I went to New York. Andrew, sensing my interests outside HUD, gave me a larger window into politics. For the 2000 Democratic presidential convention in Los Angeles, I volunteered to staff Kerry Kennedy, Andrew's then-wife. I knew the city well from my years at UCLA, and I had a great time driving Kerry around to all the fancy parties, even just standing by her side and collecting the business cards of people she met. (I know that sounds pathetic.) Thank God I soaked up that experience, because my stint at HUD was short-lived. The 2000 election cycle didn't work out for Democrats, and just seven months after I arrived in D.C., my job, like Andrew's, ended with *Bush v. Gore*. There would be no appointed positions in Washington for Democrats for four, maybe eight years, so I had to find a new route into public service. Not everybody left the city with grace. Many young disheartened Democratic staffers pried the "W" keys off their keyboards. That way their Republican replacements wouldn't be able to type the name of their new commander-in-chief: George W. Bush.

Chapter 3

So What If the Cows Outnumber Your Supporters?

A few days after I moved back to New York City, just before Christmas 2000, Jonathan and I took a walk in Central Park. The place felt magical, the ground pristine white and covered in snow, and in a secluded patch of pine trees Jonathan handed me a snowball. Before I had time to toss it toward him, he said, "Open it."

I crushed the ball in my gloves and found buried in the flakes the most beautiful diamond engagement ring. I felt so elated to know I'd be spending my life with Jonathan. Maybe returning from Washington to New York wasn't so bad after all.

The next five months were heaven. I took a job as a partner at Boies, Schiller & Flexner, David Boies's law firm, and negotiated to start in June. So I spent the next four months planning our wedding. (I love weddings, especially officiating; I've been honored to conduct ceremonies for Jonathan's brother, Simon, and his partner, Justo, as well as for two of my staffers and a couple of friends.) I also love to-do lists, so I broke down the job of planning my own wedding into a 10-point action plan:

1. dress
2. reception
3. guest list
4. rings
5. ceremony
6. invitations
7. photographer
8. band
9. flowers
10. cake

I kept a list of these ten items on an index card in my purse, noting a point person and phone number for each. We were married on April 7, 2001, at the Saint Ignatius Loyola Church in New York City, with a hundred or so family and friends. After a two-week honeymoon in Lanai, Hawaii, we came down to earth and started our new life.

One of the reasons David Boies's firm appealed to me—besides the fact that he, Jonathan Schiller, Don Flexner, and his other partners are brilliant—is that the firm took on cases of national, and sometimes even moral, importance. (David had represented Gore's campaign in the Supreme Court after the 2000 election. He most recently fought to overturn California's Proposition 8, which banned gay marriage.) Another draw: Boies's firm had an office in Albany, and that allowed me to think about moving back home.

By the time I took that job, I'd ventured so far as to tell Jonathan that I might be interested in running for something someday and I'd floated the idea of buying a house upstate. For a few years, we'd been driving up on weekends and in the summers, hiking trails at Bear Mountain, adventuring in the Catskills, eating eggs and hash at the Daily Planet Diner on Route 55, and enjoying romantic Adirondack getaways. "Who knows," I'd say to Jonathan as we were returning to the city, bouyant and relaxed. "Maybe, possibly, we could decide to live upstate full-time someday . . . ?" I was vague and indirect, unusual for me. The idea of running for office still scared me—and I worried it would scare Jonathan, too.

But Jonathan loved upstate New York, so we started house hunting, heading north most Saturday mornings to the Hudson Valley. Those weekends together, in 2002 and 2003, were some of the happiest we've shared. We looked mostly at old farmhouses and always seemed to fall in love with the most impractical ones, including a house with an ancient rainwater-drainage trench in the basement that we nicknamed "A River Runs Through It."

From the beginning, I wanted Jonathan to choose the house, since I was getting to move back home. That priority never changed, but after a while, if we liked a property, I found myself wondering what district it was in. I wanted, if possible, to buy in the 20th Congressional District, where the incumbent was John Sweeney, a Republican good ol' boy with a horrible voting record. If we bought farther south I'd have to oppose Sue Kelly—equally conservative, also with a terrible record—but I didn't want to run against a woman, given how few served in Congress. (Even today, the House of Representatives is only 18 percent women.)

About a year and a half after our wedding, I got pregnant. There's something about pregnancy that focuses the mind, even as it makes you nauseous, so along with house hunting, I started to think more practically about what it would take to run for Congress and whether I could win. One of the first people I asked for guidance was a pollster named Jefrey Pollock. Several friends had advised me that if I ever contemplated a campaign, I should talk to him first. So I called and Jefrey invited me to his office, in a modest building downtown in New York City, where the creaky elevator opened onto a huge loft space with high ceilings, industrial windows, and old wood floors. Jefrey, sitting behind his well-organized desk, said, "So, how can I help?"

"I'm thinking about running for Congress in the Twentieth Congressional District in New York," I said. He was the first person, besides Jonathan and my mother, to whom I had spoken those words. Jefrey looked a little concerned.

He walked over to his bookshelf, pulled off a thick paperback, and started reading aloud statistics about voter registration, Democratic performance numbers, and past electoral results. I didn't know what the numbers meant. He translated: In the 20th Congressional District, a Democrat could expect roughly 45 percent of the vote.

"Do you think I can win?" I asked, trying to get clarification.

Jefrey said, "No. You can't possibly win. There aren't enough Democrats in that district."

This flustered me. "What happens if I run the perfect campaign?" I felt sure Jefrey was underestimating how hard I planned to work.

"It doesn't matter," he said. "There aren't enough Democrats. The district is two-to-one Republican," meaning it had twice as many registered Republicans as Democrats.

"What happens if I raise two million dollars and really get my message out?"

Jefrey didn't budge. "It doesn't matter. That's not how campaigns actually work."

Now I was getting angry and impatient. Obviously Jefrey lacked confidence in me, which I didn't appreciate. "What happens if Sweeney gets indicted?" I asked.

Jefrey didn't miss a beat. "Well, it depends what he gets indicted for!"

When I told Jonathan about the conversation, he shrugged it off. "Don't worry," he said. "We don't know where we'll live anyway, and this is not yet relevant for us."

I was twelve weeks pregnant at the time. My due date felt like a deadline. I had a lot to do. At the top of my list was convincing the senior women in the Democratic Party that I was a worthwhile risk. That started with Judith Hope.

Judith was a legend, the first woman chair of the New York State Democratic Committee and also the founder of the Eleanor Roosevelt Legacy Committee, a group dedicated to training and supporting Democratic women to run for local office. When Judith met me for breakfast in midtown Manhattan, I could tell that she was skeptical. I was too young, too green. Learning that I was Polly Noonan's granddaughter did reassure her somewhat. (Judith loved my grandmother.) But what really won her over was when, a few months later, I filled my apartment building's reception room with seventy women under forty to raise money for the Eleanor Roosevelt Legacy. Gaining trust in politics means showing you can deliver. In some ways that event felt like my first real political triumph. Unlike at my Hillary fundraiser a few years prior, I didn't have a former first lady as my draw.

Pregnancy also turbocharged my nesting instincts. I was determined to be living in a home upstate before baby Theo arrived. Luckily, Jonathan found a perfect house in the town of Hudson: a white 1930s colonial with dark-green shutters and views of the Hudson River and the Catskills. The sellers wanted to wait to close until after Christmas, but I insisted on August. My mother served as our lawyer. Theo was born on November 8, 2003, and we were so happy to bring him to our new home.

Boies, Schiller didn't have a maternity-leave policy before I started there. So I wrote one, granting primary caregivers in the firm three months' paid leave (and also demonstrating, to myself and others, how important it is for all women to have females in leadership positions). Despite the lack of sleep, Theo's infancy, for me, was bliss. I'm not a person who likes to just relax; I prefer to do and plan things. So during quiet hours with Theo, I started to think seriously again about running for Congress. When Theo was a few months old, I finally worked up the nerve to ask Jonathan directly how he would feel about the race. I said, "Bunny, I know it's a lot to ask, and I really need this to be a family decision, but I've been thinking a lot again about running for Congress. What do you think? Do you think we could do it?"

I was still soft-pedaling the proposition because I was afraid he'd say no. The ask was huge—running would mean a massive pay cut for me, a devastating loss of privacy for our family, significant emotional discomfort for Jonathan (due in part to negative campaign ads), and a commute to Washington while we had a toddler.

Jonathan weighed the question. "I'm only going to agree if you can show me you can win," he said, meaning he could get with the idea if he could see a clear path to success. So we agreed to just keep exploring the possibility—which is a good way to do things, but not my usual modus operandi. I typically decide where I want my life to go, then figure out how I'm going to get there and build the case for why it's a good idea. Jonathan, by contrast, evaluates the pros and cons before starting out. Needless to say, he's a positive and calming influence on me.

I also called my sister, Erin, to discuss it. After I told her that I was thinking about running for Congress and that I didn't have a great chance of winning, she asked the real question: "Why do you even want to run?"

The two of us are wired very differently. She's an amazing natural parent; I need her guidance at times. She's now a yoga instructor, and before that, for work, she built a pirate ship in Baltimore Harbor, near where she lives, and rented it out for kids' birthday parties. But since that bonding moment in my early teens, we'd been sharing our truest thoughts and offering advice and unconditional love, so I told her that I felt like I needed to do more with my life. "I'm worried that when I die, God is going to ask me why I didn't do more," I said.

Erin didn't laugh. She just pointed out all the good I was doing already—for Theo, Jonathan, our family, my church, the charities I supported. But I explained that I felt like I had a wider circle of accountability, more people I needed to help, and that brought her around. Sure, she thought that I was a bit crazy. Erin would not run for elected office for all the money in the world. She dedicates her focus to a tighter, more tangible circle. But she knows me, loves me, and accepts me as I am, so she supported my election bid. To this day she talks about both of us working in the trenches. "Being a stay-at-home-parent, like being a politician, is a dirty job," she said. "But somebody has to do both. It helps if you have affinity for and love what you do."

Finally, I called Hillary Clinton. She telephoned me back one winter afternoon when a friend and I were driving home from pitching my election bid to the ten county chairs of the 20th Congressional District.

We pulled over to the side of the road so my cell wouldn't drop the call. After some small talk, Hillary got to the point. "What district are you thinking of running in?" She listened, then asked, "Who are you running against?"

Hillary was very concerned that my district was heavily Republican and that my opponent had a reputation as a mean guy. She never stated her opinion on my candidacy directly. She just asked a lot of questions that I didn't have great answers to: "What about the baby?" "What about Jonathan?"

When I hung up, I knew that she thought I should wait. A race in 2004 was premature and most likely unwinnable. Eventually, Jonathan and I agreed that Hillary's instincts were right.

To make sure I'd be ready for the following cycle, I enrolled in campaign-training school. Yes, these schools exist, and anyone can go. Most take place over a weekend and cover subjects such as how to raise money, talk to the press, build a field plan, get out the vote, what to wear and how to present yourself. In 2003, the summer before Theo was born, I attended the weeklong Women's Campaign School at Yale. Even there, I felt slightly awkward standing up and saying, "I'm considering running for Congress," because maybe only 10 percent of the women attending intended to be candidates themselves. Most planned to staff campaigns, working in finance or communications.

At the Yale training, I learned how to stay on point, how to look poised and confident, and how to keep a smile on my face even if a reporter asks a question and inside I am thinking, "Holy shit, what should I say?" I learned that you don't need everyone to like you and you shouldn't waste your time trying. You just need 50 percent of the voters, plus one.

I did a second school in the summer of 2004, through the Eleanor Roosevelt Legacy, where I learned more about organizing contacts and creating circles of supporters, from closest friends on out to acquaintances. There, I met Sam Barend, a twenty-five-year-old running for Congress in the Southern Tier of upstate New York. She was confident and excited, and I wanted to be campaigning alongside her. The third school I attended was run by the Women's Campaign Fund. There I met Jeanine Pirro, a Republican who was campaigning for attorney general. She famously lost page ten of her announcement speech and took a full thirty seconds to regain her composure, and although I didn't support her candidacy, my heart was right there with her. Both women lost but weren't broken by it, and that also felt instructive. I still feared how painful and embarrassing it would be to campaign and lose.

As I passed on the 2004 cycle and waited for the next round, in 2006, I kept my hand in politics. Through Theo's infancy, I fundraised for John Kerry and built my credibility with the doyennes of the Democratic Party. My biggest project was starting a new group under the Women's Leadership Forum for young women interested in politics, called the Women's Leadership Forum Network. I identified more than a dozen terrific young women to be on our board, placing one woman in charge of events, another in charge of policy, another in charge of outreach. I wanted each to have an important position in order to hone her leadership skills. The Women's Leadership Forum Network raised money, hosted debate-watching parties, and conducted speaking and advocacy training sessions. (Silda Spitzer attended one before her husband was elected governor, and that's where I began to respect and admire her.) I took as my job convincing higher-ups in the Democratic Party that young people's participation was just as important as older people's, even if the young ones wrote smaller checks. Our group had so much energy and so much potential that I was able to wrangle us up lots of invitations and credentials for the 2004 Democratic National Convention in Boston—hard tickets to get. Theo was eight months old at the time, so I brought him with me. While he strolled along the Charles River with a babysitter, I pumped and dumped breast milk in the hot, sweaty convention center ladies' room. If you haven't been to a political convention, they're just like big sporting events, except they're several days long and the entertainment is a parade of droning political speeches instead of athletic games. (Envious yet?) The women who traveled with me were younger—no kids yet—so each evening when I returned to the hotel with Theo, they headed to the parties. I even left them at the Fleet Center on the night of the keynote address, while I went back to my hotel room to watch the young Barack Obama on TV. I was so inspired and exhausted that I started crying and whispered to sleeping Theo, "This is such a good speech."

After the 2004 elections, Jonathan and I started looking again at a 20th Congressional District race. True to character, Jonathan wanted to see a business plan, a navigable road to success. That meant we needed a poll.

I called Jefrey Pollock again and asked him to collect data on a possible 2006 race, me versus John Sweeney, a four-term Republican incumbent. Sweeney was a tough campaigner with real financial backing. He'd helped trigger the so-called Brooks Brothers Riot that shut down the recount in Florida during the 2000 presidential election, earning the affection of President Bush (as well as the nickname Congressman Kick-Ass). But Sweeney was dogged by rumors of drunk driving and barroom fights. I was ready for what was sure to be a brutal race, if Jonathan was up for it.

The poll cost Jonathan and me $10,000, and the numbers Jefrey found were daunting. They showed us losing to Sweeney 57 percent to 14 percent. Jefrey also confirmed that Sweeney would run a nasty campaign.

But he told us his data showed that over half the voters in the district were undecided. All the Democrats would likely vote Democrat, but only half the Republicans would likely vote Republican, so if we did well with the Independents we could win. Voters in the district weren't loyal to Sweeney.

That was good enough for Jonathan. Now I just had to convince everybody else. My mother—who understood my district and, more important, me—thought my decision to run was fantastic. Erin and a few friends knew enough not to underestimate me or stand in my way. Nearly everyone else just humored me and said, "Good luck."

Still, I asked everybody in my network for their support.

Politics is not for the timid or shy. First, I went back to Hillary and was grateful and happy when she agreed to review Jefrey's poll. We made a phone date and when I called at the appointed time from my campaign office in Albany, she had already talked to Rahm Emanuel, then the head of the Democratic Congressional Campaign Committee. Rahm, she said, thought I was a "great candidate." Karen Persichilli Keogh, one of her closest political advisors, whom she'd also talked to, advised the race would be "an uphill climb." (KPK, as she's affectionately known, later worked on my first Senate campaign and was an invaluable advisor.) Of course, Hillary was concerned about Theo, our recent move to Hudson, my limited experience in public service, and my opponent's reputation. Still, what she focused on most was why I wanted to run and how I would feel if I lost. "You should only run if your heart is one hundred percent in it," she said. We talked about my platform, messaging, and how I should present myself. She described the decision of whether or not to run as a "close call."

She shared personal stories about some of President Clinton's early races, including one where he came from twenty-four points behind to lose by only three, and how he used that opportunity to establish a strong reputation to win down the road. She couldn't have been more gracious or kind, offering to talk through the race as I made my decision, to explore other avenues for service if I didn't run, and to help and support me no matter what. (And she and President Clinton did, with fundraising events, stumping in the district, and speaking at huge rallies just before the election.) Her last few words of advice were that I should only run if I was "taking it on out of conviction," and there would be no guarantees. Campaigns could be nasty stuff, she said. I would have to have a thick skin. If I got in the game, I would have to play to win.

I definitely wanted to win, and I do have very thick skin. I knew that I was ready, especially with Hillary in my corner.

Next, I asked every woman I knew who was very experienced in politics to meet one-on-one. I always showed up promptly, neatly dressed, and with a smile on my face and a notebook in hand. The tone of most of the encounters, at least early on, was polite, kind of thrilling (for me), and mildly discouraging. Ellen Chesler, who'd worked on campaigns for a long time, gave me a list of ten more people to call. Susan Thomases, one of Hillary's longtime friends and advisors, asked, "Do you know all your neighbors in Hudson yet?"

Such a simple question. I shook my head. Susan said, "When a reporter knocks on your neighbor's door and asks about you, and your neighbor says, 'I've never met her,' that's a bad story."

Jane Harman, who at the time was a congresswoman from California, asked, "What's your platform? What can you do before you run to elevate your name statewide? Can you get on some boards?" She didn't think my chances were good, but she offered to throw me a fundraiser anyway.

In August 2005, I registered as a candidate and got to work on the next item on my to-do list: getting to know as many people in the district as possible. A friend would say, "My mother has a bridge group that comes to her house on Thursday evenings. Would you like to meet them?" I'd say, "Yes! Thank you!" Then I'd go, sit down, and speak with the women, asking about their concerns and writing down their answers in blue felt-tip pen on white index cards: SOCIAL SECURITY, TAX BREAKS FOR COLLEGE TUITION, NEW NATIONAL HEALTHCARE MODEL. (This was before Obamacare.) I kept those cards in my purse, just as I had my wedding-planning index card. They became my external brain—a necessity, because I forget things I don't write down.

I also set out to meet with leaders of three groups: labor, the Democratic Congressional Campaign Committee, and EMILY's List. For the first, I met with Suzy Ballantyne, one of the top figures in the New York State AFL-CIO. I figured Suzy would be tough and dismiss me outright, but she listened politely to my then-not-very-polished presentation on why I thought I could beat John Sweeney and said, to my great pleasure, "You know, Kirsten, I think John Sweeney is full of shit. I will help you."

Next hurdle: the Democratic Congressional Campaign Committee (or D triple-C, as insiders call it), run at the time by Rahm Emanuel. True to his reputation, Rahm was a hard-ass and a skeptic. He kept giving me outrageous fundraising goals, assuming I'd fall short and thus give him an excuse to bar me from his Red to Blue program, aimed at turning Republican districts Democratic. But I jumped through every hoop, rang every bell, called every number of every contact, and eventually Rahm ran out of reasons not to support me.

That left winning the support of EMILY's List, which I knew I couldn't do unless I had labor and the DCCC on my side. They were the toughest to win over, but when I did, EMILY's List was invaluable—helping me with staffing, training my finance team, and sending out emails and letters to their hundreds of thousands of supporters, explaining why they should help me.

In January 2006, a month after my thirty-ninth birthday, I announced my candidacy to a small gathering at the historic and charming Tin Ballroom in Hudson. Later that afternoon, I drove to Saratoga and announced my candidacy again. The next morning, I announced a third time in a maple barn in Delaware County, surrounded by farmers. I was still so green that in Saratoga I spoke for twenty-five minutes (at least fifteen minutes longer than I should have), irritating all the politicians who were standing behind me, including Eliot Spitzer, then attorney general. Afterward, reporters pushed cameras in my face for the first time in my life. Thankfully, I remembered my media training from campaign school: One, smile. Two, breathe. Three, keep it simple. Four, smile again.

Our campaign was so scrappy. My grandmother had died the week that Theo was born, but our family hadn't sold her house, so it was a low-cost (and therefore perfect) place for my scruffy band of staffers to live. I imagine she would have loved the energy and chaos. Between five and ten people lived at that house at any given time, some camping out for weeks in sleeping bags on the old white carpet, so focused on my campaign—as opposed to, say, vacuuming—that my mother had to have the entire place recarpeted when my staffers left. Ross Offinger, then twenty-three years old, who started as my deputy finance manager and still works with me today, took a job on my campaign so he could move out of his childhood bedroom at his parents' Massachusetts home. He ended up living at my grandmother's for over a year. As our unofficial dean of housing, he installed a foosball table in the living room and, predictably, often woke the whole house at 2:00 A.M. by yelling, "Score!"

My treasurer, Anne Bradley, who is now my deputy chief of staff, was at a very different place in her life. When she started, she was a principal at Ernst & Young, working for them part-time and remotely while doing her campaign duties for free. At a certain point, being the only real adult in my grandmother's house, she couldn't take the collegiate-style crash pad anymore and moved in with my mother. I really appreciated her company, as the average age of my campaign staff was around twenty-five.

Bill Hyers, my gruff but experienced campaign manager and Anne's boss, knew how to keep a campaign focused and disciplined, spending money only when he knew it would earn us voters. Toilet paper and other supplies didn't qualify.

My role, at the beginning, was to spend days on end talking to people who didn't think I could win. I called every name of every contact anybody would give me, putting small check marks next to each to remind myself how many times I'd already called. Anybody who was willing, I drew into the campaign. I asked people to throw coffee get-togethers where I could meet voters (and write down their concerns on index cards). If throwing a coffee seemed like too big a request, I'd ask if they could bring muffins to an event someone else was hosting. If bringing muffins seemed like a hassle, I asked if they'd be willing to attend and bring along a friend. People like to help—it's human nature. From tax lawyers I asked tax-policy advice; from teachers, their thoughts on education policy. Contributing made people feel like part of my campaign, and that made them emotionally invested in it.

Sweeney hurled everything he had at the race, including a bunch of ridiculous lies. He said that I'd wasted billions of dollars at HUD, that I was a war profiteer, that I wanted to eliminate the child tax credit, and that I was an out-of-touch Manhattanite who hired a maid to polish my silver. He ran campaign ads criticizing all the men close to me—my dad, my brother, my father-in-law, and my husband. My attitude was "Fuck 'em." One of the lessons I'd learned from my grandmother was to ignore negative press. Politics, she taught me, is a sport, just like football. You put on your protective gear, get out on the field, and hit your opponent as hard as you can. You should expect your opponent to do the same.

Jonathan, on the other hand, was enraged. "This is complete bullshit," he said upon seeing Sweeney's ads. He turned the TV off in September and didn't turn it back on until November, when the election was over. He told my staff to remove his name from the daily email of campaign clips. Being British, he was appalled that political ads in the United States were held to no standard for truth.

To counteract the ugliness, Jonathan and Theo made huge wooden signs with the words GILLIBRAND 4 CHANGE or FARMERS FOR GILLIBRAND painted in red, white, and blue. They then surprised me by placing the signs on lawns along my drive to the campaign office. Lawn signs, I knew by that point, are fairly useless in swaying voters, but they sure did make me feel good. Most satisfying: Sweeney's negative attack strategy appeared to be backfiring. All by myself, standing on a street corner talking about Iraq policy, I wasn't that captivating to voters. But once Sweeney started hurling insults at me, people felt offended and paid attention to the race. Nobody likes a man who maligns a new mother. If Sweeney had had the restraint to ignore me, he probably would have won.

Campaigns are trials of perseverance. Every day, you wake up, examine what other people think of you (never a recipe for happiness), and talk to voters who don't like you, because if you only talk to your supporters, you'll never change anybody's mind and win more votes. I met with every editorial board of every conservative newspaper, eager to convince them I was hardworking and sincere. If we'd planned an event and not enough people RSVP'd yes, we'd call hundreds more until we had a respectable number of attendees. Jonathan tried to keep up morale by regularly supplying campaign headquarters with pizza and beer—and toilet paper when needed.

The last two weeks before the election were really dramatic. For the first time I had a lead over Sweeney and could see a clear path to victory. Then an important local newspaper ran a police report raising serious doubts about Sweeney's character and credibility. This led the most prominent paper in the most Republican part of the district to retract its endorsement of Sweeney and back me. Adding to the cascade of good luck, Hillary Clinton's birthday was a week and a half before the election, and when Bill asked her what she wanted as a gift, she said she wanted him to go campaign for me.

This was far beyond anything I'd ever imagined. Hillary had already been so generous, attending two rallies and two fundraisers. President Clinton had been to the district on my behalf just a few weeks before. Now Hillary asked for this present, and Bill delivered. That day still seems like a dream. The Monday before the Tuesday vote, the president flew in to the Glens Falls airport, where he took the podium and said, charming as ever, "A few days ago it was my wife's birthday. I said, 'What do you want me to do for your birthday?' and she said, 'I want you to go to upstate New York and help Kirsten Gillibrand win that election.' And then she said, 'And while you're up there, you might get me a vote or two if you can.'"

I was bursting with gratitude and excitement—President Clinton, here again, for my campaign. The pictures from that day are hysterical. I look as amped up as a child who's just been fed five spoonfuls of sugar and given a hundred balloons. After the president's speech, while he signed photos and books for supporters, I chatted with him about other young Democrats and the 2008 presidential race. He took Barack Obama very seriously. I was less savvy at the time, so fond of Hillary that I told the president I was positive she was going to win.

He smiled. The president clearly shared my adoration and respect, but he also said he thought Obama was a very good candidate.

"But there's no way Hillary will lose. She's fantastic and she's so qualified," I said.

The president kept smiling. I'm sure he hoped that I was right.

On election day, when I woke up, I felt a little strange. At that point in a campaign, you've either done the hard work or you haven't, and all you can do is wait for the votes and see. Theo, in a bright-red sweater, joined me at the polls that morning. As soon as I pushed back the voting-booth curtain, he shouted to a scrum of cameras, "Mommy's going to win!"

After that I drove home, changed into jeans, and got my hair done. Then, as a family, we meandered north. Once in Saratoga, I stopped on Broadway and bought a new outfit—a gray suit with lavender pinstripes and a purple shell. I knew it wouldn't go well with the campaign banners, but I liked it, so I didn't care. (It also didn't have Theo's breakfast on it, like most of my suits did.) At dinner, family and friends retold funny campaign stories, relived the president's visit, and kicked around possible tricks Sweeney still might have in store.

Finally we headed to the hotel to watch the returns. The moment we checked in, I hit a wall. I'd been campaigning almost constantly for two years. I collapsed on the bed and fell asleep. In another room, Jonathan, Ross Offinger, Bill Hyers, and Sean Gavin, my grassroots campaign expert, scoured the numbers, their energy ramping up by the hour, until the polls closed at 9:00 P.M. and results started to trickle in. The early returns from some of my toughest counties were positive, so I pulled myself together and joined Jonathan and the others as my team's excitement began to build. The whole country was watching the election closely, as the congressional majority had a chance to switch from Republican to Democratic. The networks called our district at around 11:30 P.M., just around the same time the House was called.

I raced down to the hotel ballroom, thanked my staff, family, friends, and supporters profusely, and then my phone started ringing nonstop. Hillary Clinton. Bill Clinton. Dozens of volunteers. Donors. All my old friends. I felt just like I had during my wedding: thrilled, drained, overcome by gratitude and love.

The next day was Theo's third birthday, and we had a huge family celebration at my mother's house. During the party, CNN called to invite me on one of their shows for the next morning. I wanted to say yes. I thought I should have said yes, but I felt utterly wiped out. I'd worked so hard for so long, I needed to be home with Jonathan and Theo, so I declined.

The next morning, while drinking my tea, I turned on the TV to see what I'd missed, and there was Gabby Giffords. This was the first time I'd really watched her—her warm smile, her smart, compassionate eyes. Like me, she'd won a Red to Blue race and was heading to Washington to be a freshman in Congress. I couldn't wait to meet her. We seemed to have so much in common already, though obviously she was tougher than I was. I was home on the couch in my sweatpants, and she was before the cameras, hopeful, tireless, and poised.

Chapter 4

The Best Lobbyist I Ever Met Was a Twelve-Year-Old Girl

The election results meant that the Democrats had taken over the House, and that meant that Nancy Pelosi was now speaker, and as speaker, she changed the rules. Congress would now meet five days a week, as opposed to three, and that meant my family plans needed to change. Instead of the family staying put in Hudson and me commuting to Washington Tuesday mornings and home Thursday nights, we would all move. I was only slightly rattled by this. I wanted to be with my family full-time. Plus, I thrive on chaos. Enormous changes at the last minute don't bother me much. But Jonathan is different. He likes order and a long-term plan. And he didn't have a job in D.C. During the election, we'd both assumed that, win or lose, our family life would remain fairly unaltered. My mother would pitch in with Theo when I was traveling, and it wouldn't be a big deal. But these changes were a big deal—a very big deal. This was lousy news for Jonathan. He had a great job in venture capital in New York. Who wants to be pulled from his life on short notice to follow someone else's dream?

Two other factors made that first week more unnerving. First, as soon as I arrived in Washington, I started getting lobbied about whom I would support for Democratic majority leader. Nancy Pelosi was the speaker; that was set. But John Murtha, a congressman from Pennsylvania, and Steny Hoyer, a congressman from Maryland, both wanted to be her number two.

Steny Hoyer had campaigned for me in my district. Rahm had called him last minute to see if he could fly to New York State on Sunday to stump for a new candidate. Steny had tried to decline politely, saying, "I'd love to, but I really have to check my schedule."

Rahm said, "I already spoke to your scheduler! Great—you're free Sunday." So Steny had flown up.

He won the hearts of Albany and many votes on my behalf, and as he was leaving he'd asked a favor. "If you win, Kirsten, which I know you're going to do, will you support me for majority leader?"

"Absolutely!" I'd said. "I promise I'll support you!"

Now here I was in my hotel room, my first week in Washington, surrounded by mugs, bottles of wine, books, and chocolates, gifts from both the pro-Murtha and pro-Hoyer camps. I was screwed. Nancy Pelosi supported Murtha. That meant, on my first day of work, I was going to have to walk into her office and refuse to vote with her. This was like telling a new boss on the first day of work that you don't agree with the company's business plan.

Sure enough, Nancy called me into her office, which is manned by a security detail and myriad staff members, and told me how much she'd like me to support Murtha. I said, "Madam Speaker, I respect you so much. I'm going to vote for you for speaker. I think you're wonderful. But I support Steny."

The consternation that flashed on her face! I realized I needed to acquire some better political skills fast. But I've never regretted my support of Steny, ever.

The second thing that happened that first week was even darker and more stressful. I was sitting in the House chambers, expecting an orientation meeting that would include basics such as how the congressional computer system works and where the bathroom is. Instead, I found myself listening to a senior congressman's heart-to-heart about what he'd learned from his decades in Washington. At the time, I was already feeling a little blue. Jonathan and Theo were with my father in the Virgin Islands, on a trip my father planned before the election, as none of us realized that if I won I'd need to be in D.C. this week. The night before, I had stood around a cocktail party, talking to no one. So far, Congress was lonely. Now this older congressman was saying, "Most members of Congress's marriages end in divorce. Most members of Congress—their children do not even speak to them, or they hate them." The room grew very quiet. "You are the only one who can protect your family here, and that means putting them first when you schedule your time. You're going to have to stand in front of your twenty-two-year-old scheduler, whose job it is to schedule every minute of your day, and protect your family. Nobody else will. You don't want to look up years from now and find your family is gone." To this day, that was the single most important piece of advice I have been given about serving in Congress.

So I set to work building an office consistent with my values. I knew from the start that I needed to find a way to schedule myself that would keep my young family intact. I also knew I wanted transparency. To me that meant posting my earmark requests, official daily meetings, and personal financial disclosures online. Anybody could Google anything these days. Why should the inner workings of my office not be available for constituents to see?

My chief of staff, Jess Fassler, thought this was crazy and would invite needless criticism and attack. "Of course you can't do that," he said. "Nobody does that!"

"Of course I can," I said. "If I can't defend taking a meeting, I shouldn't be taking that meeting."

So I created my Sunlight Report and posted my official daily meetings on the Web at the end of each day, so voters could see with whom I was meeting and know who had my ear. My colleagues didn't like this much. One teased me on the House floor. "We're having a conversation now. Is that a meeting? Are you going to post it on your website?" I understood the provocation but forged ahead because it was the right thing to do. *The New York Times* called my efforts "a quiet touch of revolution," and within two years Speaker Pelosi mandated that everyone had to post their earmark requests online.

Around this time, I realized that almost everything I thought I knew about being a congressperson was wrong. I thought the job would be wonky, that I'd spend the bulk of my time studying foreign policy and researching ideas for achieving energy independence. I presumed that to succeed I'd need encyclopedic knowledge of all the bills on the floor, that I'd win debates with data. But I quickly learned that representing people is much more about empathy and knowing what they're going through. The job is to listen and care. Only then do the laws, facts, and figures begin to matter.

I decided against doing only typical town-hall events and instead tried to seek out people who wouldn't normally approach a politician. This meant standing around grocery stores, coffee shops, and farm stands. In early 2008, I planned a Congress on Your Corner at a garden center in Glens Falls, a town in the northern corner of my district. Among the potting soil, flowers, and trees, I just started talking. "Hi, everybody. I'm Kirsten Gillibrand. I'm your new congresswoman and just wanted to know what's on your mind—what's bothering you, what you're worried about."

About twenty-five people gathered around, and together we talked about their issues. Some were worried about the economy, others about Iraq. A few wanted more accountability in Washington in general. I addressed their concerns as best I could: "Here's where we stand on Iraq"; "I know the economy's tough"; "Yes, Washington's broken." When the crowd started to dissipate, two women in their mid-thirties stepped forward.

Both looked nervous. One had tears in her eyes. The more emotional woman spoke up first. "Mrs. Gillibrand, I just got a bill from the government for twenty-five dollars because I receive child support." She scanned my face for a reaction. "Twenty-five dollars might not seem like a lot of money to you, but to me it is. It's money for lunches for my three boys for a week." Her voice grew more forceful as she talked. "I don't know why the state is billing me. You have to do something about this. I can't afford it and I don't think it's fair."

I didn't know quite how to react at first. This sounded terrible, but I wasn't sure what I could do about it. "That sounds awful," I finally said. "Let me find out what's going on. I promise I will get back to you."

It wasn't enough. These women weren't satisfied and rightly so. This mother had trusted me with her story. She had told me what she cared and worried about. I felt her anger, even empathized with it, but I hadn't done anything about it. I asked the woman to write down her name on a scrap of paper I found in my purse. I needed to find a way to help her and help others like her. That was my job as her representative, right?

This woman and her boys were the first thing I told Jonathan about when I saw him that night—and that $25 bill and those lunches are still in my mind. The first bill I introduced when I entered the Senate was to stop states from charging recipients of child support for the overhead (that's what the $25 bill had been for). What higher priority should we have as a country than feeding our children?

And what could be a more stupid way to go about implementing the program than to charge the bureaucratic costs to the very people who need the money? I still battle the constant cutting of food stamps, and every time I hear a story about a mother unable to make lunch, or breakfast, or dinner for her children, I want to explode with rage. How, in this country, the wealthiest country in the world, can we allow children to go hungry? This year's cuts to the food-stamps program would have erased $90 from the monthly budget of three hundred thousand New York families if our governor had not intervened. It truly disturbs me how little some leaders care. Few lobby for food stamps, because the people who need them aren't in positions of power. The logic is sad and twisted.

Please believe me: Your story matters. Keep telling it until it falls on the right ears. Once, a veteran who lost a limb in Vietnam told me, "When I strap on my leg, I strap on my patriotism. Why isn't the VA supporting me?" Those two sentences moved my office to work until we got him $60,000 in benefits and back pay. This story also opened my eyes to the backlog of veterans' claims caused by the chronic underfunding of the Veterans Administration.

I also hear stories from mayors, church leaders, activists, philanthropists, and community leaders about all kinds of suffering we must address. "Our food bank sees more families and more children than ever before, but less food is coming in, because of the tough economy. Could you help?" Or, "My church runs an after-school program for at-risk youth, and we're running out of funding. Can you get us federal money to stay open?" When people raise their voices, they give leaders opportunities to truly help and serve.

As I settled in to my new job, my constituents' voices defined my agenda. Good ideas don't come from Washington. They come from individuals willing to share their experiences and needs. About a year into my term, I met with a woman named Kate Miller whose son, Cody, had recently committed suicide. She sat in my office, on my blue couch, with all her dignity, sadness, and rage, and told me how her son had taken medicine for allergies that she believed left him so severely depressed that he took his own life.

My mind flashed to Theo. I tried to comfort Kate and I thanked her for her bravery in telling me her story, but mostly I just cried with her and absorbed some of her pain. I couldn't imagine what it would feel like to lose a son to suicide. I could only inch myself a few steps down the horrible road before my brain started to rebel. But I felt the full measure of Kate's need to make her loss mean something, for Cody's life and death to produce a shred of good in the world.

Kate wanted help with a campaign to force the FDA to put clearer labels on drugs that can cause depression, specifically drugs that can cause depression in children. I was on board, 100 percent. "I've learned that people will forget what you said, people will forget what you did, but people will never forget how you made them feel," Maya Angelou has been quoted as saying. That's certainly true for me.

Women kept coming—mothers trying to solve problems for their children, parents trying to prevent others from suffering the same loss. Sometimes I met the children themselves, and, let me tell you, there is no more powerful lobbyist in the world than a twelve-year-old girl. Early one Saturday morning at a bagel shop, after my scheduler had put off the request for months, I met a group of mothers with daughters who had type 1 diabetes. The girls didn't say much. They didn't have to—just the basic facts told me a story of pain and courage. They wore their insulin monitors under their school clothes, their soccer uniforms, even their prom dresses. They refused to be afraid or sidelined by a disease. Their mothers gave the details.

"My daughter has to get injections in her thigh every few hours."

"Every time I let my sixteen-year-old daughter go out for a night with her friends, I just pray she'll remember to check her blood sugar levels when it gets late."

You can drop a dozen binders full of white papers on my desk, and the stack won't be as effective as a single human being willing to speak honestly about her life. Of course I knew about type 1 diabetes before that day, but my knowledge was unemotional and abstract. Now I see specific faces when I think of type 1 diabetes. Faces make people respond.

Sometimes it's just a matter of daring to speak and letting the world do the rest of the work. Imagine an infant in a drop-side crib dying while sleeping, because he can't breathe. Now imagine that baby's parents telling you about losing that baby. When they demand action, you want to deliver. I met a roomful of parents who'd lost an infant. They stood with photos of their dead children. Some held other children's hands. How could you have an ounce of empathy, hear such a story, and not be moved to act? The very afternoon I met those parents, we started working to change crib-safety regulations. Drop-side cribs were banned within nine months.

That first year, as I found my way in Congress, I realized I needed to brush up on my listening skills at home, too. Our move to Washington was hard—on me *and* my marriage. I had a new job; Jonathan didn't; and we were trying to find our legs with a toddler in a new city. We started having the same argument over and over. I'd say, "What's wrong?"

Jonathan would say, "I have no job and I hate D.C."

I appreciated Jonathan's viewpoint. We lived in a soulless suburb. It wasn't the right place for us, and we needed a change. I could see that, but it took me at least a year to figure out that racing 100 miles an hour to do my job well was leaving no time for us. We tried to make a night out together each week a priority, to really talk and listen to each other. (We still do this every Saturday.) But when you're new to a city, even finding a sitter can seem insurmountable, and the best intentions fall through. It's humbling how hard it can be to do at home the things that we know we must do at work: Be patient and courteous; listen; value opposing views. Eventually we moved from Arlington, Virginia, to Capitol Hill, and Jonathan found a job he liked. I also started telling people that we wanted to make new friends in D.C., and that led to dinner parties that included Brits, which Jonathan greatly enjoyed. Perhaps best of all, we sank into our daily life. I made a point of traveling solo more, and we reduced our family's trips to Hudson from every weekend to once a month. Theo started playing T-ball and soccer on the Hill, and I made of point of keeping Jonathan top of mind.

Marriage is difficult, especially in a busy life. When you're a parent, your children need you to survive, but when you're married, your spouse seems able to fend for himself. So that relationship gets back-burnered. Then weeks pass, then months, and you're having fewer ups in your marriage and far too many downs. I know that I need Jonathan and that he needs me, but when we don't express those needs, both of us become resentful, and our relationship suffers. I try to follow the rule: Love as you'd like to be loved. When I need some TLC, I offer some to Jonathan. Most of the time, that's reflected back.

Still, that first summer I was in Congress, I was stressed and preoccupied, and one day Jonathan blurted out, "Your job is the reason we don't have more kids!"

Jonathan realized this was unfair, but it was a legitimate issue. Like every other couple building a family alongside two careers, we had many factors to consider relative to the timing of a second child. Age and travel topped my list, but the truth is I wanted another baby, too. I had just been feeling buried in our day-to-day life and not communicating well. "We can have more kids!" I told Jonathan.

I tracked my cycles (sparing my reserved, English-born husband the details) and planned a vacation at Elk Lake in the Adirondacks at just the right time. After a few days of long hikes and TV-free evenings, I came home pregnant with Henry.

At work, my own voice emerged, as well. At the beginning of the term, Speaker Pelosi put five additional women on the House Armed Services Committee. Given that she'd already put several there, this created a seismic gender shift. Early on, we had some hearings about military readiness. Typically, military-readiness hearings revolve around how many aircraft or ships we need to build or how our nation's capabilities compare to other countries' around the world. Gabby Giffords and I both thought about readiness in different terms: Were the men and women in the military as physically and mentally ready as possible to do their jobs?

An army doctor who screened soldiers before redeployment had told Gabby that he believed 70 percent of service members he was seeing needed immediate counseling, and most weren't getting it. They needed more mental-health treatment for PTSD or just more time at home. Gabby used this doctor's observations to challenge Secretary of Defense Bob Gates on how well the military was caring for its personnel. Whenever she raised an issue like that, I'd think, "Thank God someone is saying this." When it was my turn, I'd cite the high rates of divorce, domestic violence, and suicide in the United States military. Tag-teaming like that, we built a narrative that the generals began to hear: A ready military requires a ready personnel. We must do more for our troops' physical and mental health.

I know raising one's voice can be intimidating. So I want to share a few ideas about what I've found to be important over the years.

One: Don't wait to tell your story. Sometimes in life it's better to let your emotions settle. But when you want to tell a story that moves people, urgency works in your favor. Raw is okay. Let your feelings show.

Two: Believe others will care. Yes, there's good reason to be cynical about an awful lot of people in Washington and in the rest of the world. But more people are listening than you might expect. My office, just like the office of every other senator and congressperson, logs every call we receive. We want to know our constituents' concerns. It's also important to remember that you don't have to win over everybody. Let the cynics live in their small closed world. You just need to find that one right person who listens, cares, and can help.

Three: Persistence works. Call again. Email again. Stand in the back of the conference for three hours to get that two minutes of face time with the person who you think can make a difference. Those moms and their daughters with type 1 diabetes asked for a meeting for nine months. People notice and admire tenacity. Your effort will pay off in the end.

Four: Use the platform you've got. Maybe you'd like to make your point in the Opinion Pages of *The New York Times,* but if that's not happening, get the word out however you can. Who knows who will read the letter to the editor you write to your local paper, or even who will read your tweets? If you don't try, you can't succeed. This is really a case of the perfect being the enemy of the good. It's worth the time and effort, even if the venue seems silly or embarrassing. Speaking up is the essential first step.

I say this having been on both sides the equation: the person listening and the person speaking up. I am not scared to talk to anyone—Jon Stewart, Barbara Walters—but I'm starstruck and full of nerves when talking to the president. (I'm also sure I'd be tongue-tied talking to Tina Fey. I have a huge girl crush on her.) Over the years, I've had a few chances to speak to Presidents Bush, Clinton, and Obama. Each time, it's just been for a minute or two, and I always try to use those minutes to say something important. I haven't always succeeded. When I met George W. Bush, I had nothing productive to say, so I stuttered and just thanked him for his service. When I met President Clinton for the first time, at a fundraiser for him, I mostly blushed and offered my gratitude for his leadership and advocacy. But I became much more focused when I was running for office. Anytime I got a minute with Bill Clinton, I was strategic and asked him for help. "A ten-minute stop-by at the event would be ideal!" Cheeky, I know, but essential.

As a sitting senator, I've learned to use every second I get with the president wisely. If I have his ear, I have an obligation to my constituents to advocate for them. Now every time I know I'm going to see President Obama, I have a mission. Emotionally, I'm sometimes conflicted about this, because I'm sure that me advocating is the last thing he wants to hear. But as much as I would like it if President Obama always enjoyed my company, that's not a luxury I have. My job is to be a public servant. Those moments with him are extremely valuable.

Before I see the president—which doesn't just happen by coincidence, as it does with normal people—I think through exactly what I'm going to say. I even make contingency plans: "Here's my Plan A pitch if I get thirty seconds; here's my Plan B if I get a minute; here's my Plan C if I get two minutes." I always know my ask, and I always raise my hand when the president comes to our caucus meetings. There are plenty of times I'd rather blend into the crowd and not add a mountain of stress to my life, but I know how much speaking up matters. People trust me with their stories. It's my job to be their conduit.

That doesn't mean I haven't had some awkward moments. In 2010, the White House Christmas party happened to be right before the vote on the 9/11 healthcare bill, an issue that pulled on my heart and sense of justice as fiercely as anything had in my life. I'd promised the first responders and their families that I'd fight for them with everything I had. So there I was, in a blue strapless gown, standing in an endless line to wish President Obama a merry Christmas. Jonathan wasn't there; he doesn't like work parties (though he does love the congressional spouses events, and all the congressional spouses love him back). So my date was my chief of staff, Jess.

We decided we would use the holiday face time to lobby.

For the hour Jess and I stood in line, I kept second-guessing myself, asking whether Jess thought it was rude or obnoxious to spend my thirty seconds with the president at the Christmas party to urge him to throw his weight behind ensuring that our 9/11 first responders got their due.

"Do you really think it's okay to bring up my bill?"

"Yes, Kirsten, you should bring up the bill," Jess said patiently, at first.

"I'll ask him to call Senator Enzi—he's still considering whether to support the bill."

"Good call," Jess said.

"Is it rude?" I asked, feeling insecure again. Lobbying here among the fancy Christmas trees was clearly off script.

"I don't know," Jess said.

"Let's go for it."

"Yup."

Finally I got to the front of the line, to our commander in chief in his tuxedo and Michelle Obama, impeccably dressed as always, in a red ball gown. I didn't even leave the president an inch to say, "Merry Christmas." I just gulped down a chestful of air and started talking a mile a minute. "Mr. President, I'm working really hard on the 9/11 healthcare bill, and I really need your help, and if you could just call Senator Enzi—"

The president broke into a bemused smile. "Kirsten . . . Kirsten . . . happy holidays." His body language urged me to please slow down.

A second later, Jess and I had our picture taken with the president and the first lady. Then my presidential face time was done. I still have that photo in my office. In it, Jess looks a little beleaguered, and the skin on my chest is bright red, which is what happens to me when I'm nervous. But I did my best, and I'd do the same thing over again.

I even did it today. I spoke to the president for ten minutes on sexual assault in the military. He didn't intend our phone call to run that long or to be so substantive, but I didn't let him hang up with me just listening and saying, "Yes, sir." Instead, as he was winding down, I told the president the story of a survivor of military sexual assault and urged him to meet her and her husband for only five minutes. I sensed that the president needed to go. (I've retained my finely tuned ear from all those childhood debates with my father.) I guessed I had fifteen seconds left, so I pressed to tell the president one more thing: The Department of Defense's panel on the status of women in the military had just endorsed every aspect of my bill.

It's not enjoyable when your advocacy makes others feel ambushed or uncomfortable. But sometimes it's necessary, especially when fighting for moral issues. Many felt uncomfortable with the idea of repealing Don't Ask, Don't Tell. Some still resist investing in food for America's hungry—the whole topic makes them defensive and angry. Change is hard. People feel threatened; sometimes they lash out. Malala Yousafzai was shot in the head because she would not back down in fighting the Taliban and demanding education for girls. She came through that experience more powerful and clear-voiced than ever, saying, "I raise up my voice—not so that I can shout, but so that those without a voice can be heard."

You may never push something so far or so dramatically, but any one voice can spark change—never doubt it.

Chapter 5

Let's Clean Up the Sticky Floor

At the beginning of this year, I walked into Henry's kindergarten classroom, and his good friend Nico's mom, Julie, said, "You're gonna love Henry's smile project!" The kids had written notes saying what made them smile. Nico's answer, Julie told me, was literal: "Laughing." I found Henry's card and opened it: "My Mom." So sweet. This was one of those moments I relish as a parent, because I needed it so badly. Nine out of ten times, if you ask a mother how it's going, the honest answer (if she gives it) is, "Um, barely holding it together."

I do a lot of thinking and talking about the needs of American families, and as most of you know, on good days, for the majority of us, family life is an absurdist sitcom. Mine typically starts between 6:00 and 6:30 A.M., when Henry runs into my room and jumps on the bed. Almost always, I still feel exhausted when I get up. I make my kids breakfast, let them watch cartoons while I pack their lunches, throw in a load of laundry or dishes, and check that their homework is done—and if it isn't, I frantically supervise while trying to get dressed. Then, before I've even done what many women would consider a halfway-decent job with hair and makeup, I look over, see that it's 8:00 A.M., and yell, "WE HAVE TO LEAVE!" Theo likes to be early to school. But at this point, inevitably, I realize that one or both children haven't yet brushed their teeth or grabbed their coat, and when I ask them to hurry up please, Theo says, irked, "Mom, why are you always making us laaate?!" This sums up my life with a five-year-old, a ten-year-old, and a husband who works in New York City Monday through Friday while I'm solo with the kids in D.C. Few of my colleagues know what "balance" really looks like. They might see me with a child or two on any given evening, and they think it's sweet. But if they saw or heard the before and after, my guess is that they'd be frightened or concerned.

America is full of people like me who know esoteric trivia like the fact that I can drive from my office to my kids' school to the soccer field and back to the office in twenty-two minutes if I hit all the lights. People who believe in family dinner but feed their kids burgers or slices of pizza in the backseats of cars because it's the only way to get one to a piano lesson and the other to his baseball game and still get both fed.

I knew the juggle was coming, but I didn't fully appreciate it until May 14, 2008, when I was sitting—and sitting and sitting, for twelve hours straight—in a House Armed Services Committee mark-up meeting, very pregnant with Henry. This was an annual event to authorize legislation, and I was uncomfortable and wishing the waves of pain and cramping would just go away. Still, I used my dinner break to drop by a Hillary fundraiser. I didn't realize that I'd been in pre-labor all day until my water broke at 2:00 A.M.

That morning, Theo came to the hospital. I was tired and sore from a C-section but so happy to have him there. At four and a half, in a blue-and-white rugby shirt and pink cheeks, he was just growing out of his toddler days and so proud to hold his new baby brother on his lap all by himself. I was deep in the private hormonal bliss of having created a beautiful four-person family when, several hours later, as I lay in bed in my flowered pajamas, a high-ranking general came to visit. (Henry was born in a military hospital, and the general was part of the administration.) I was more than a little shocked to have work and family lines blurred so thoroughly so soon. I thanked the general profusely for the excellent care and kept smiling and holding my breath until he left.

Before long, I was home and pushing Henry's stroller down to Lincoln Park, just a few blocks from our rented house on Constitution Avenue. My mother came to visit; my father and his wife, Gwenn, came to visit. Jonathan's parents, Sydney and Angela, who live in London, stayed for three months. After 10:00 P.M. and 2:00 A.M. feedings, Henry would wake up hungry again around 5:00 A.M. I tried to have him fed and back to sleep in time to make Theo breakfast and get him ready for school. I kept my workload to a minimum (as my own boss, I could) but called in most days. When I was a child, during our family vacations, my mother would phone her secretary at 5:00 P.M. each evening to go through the mail and make sure nothing was amiss. That same approach kept me sane. If I kept a light touch on the office, I felt my life was under control.

Three and a half weeks after Henry's birth, I began seeing votes and meetings that I didn't want to miss, so I began adding them back: a meeting about the 9/11 first responders, a vote for the farm bill, a briefing on Afghanistan, a vote for unemployment insurance. At the time, it didn't feel strange to be thinking about foreign policy, milk pricing, and Henry's napping schedule all at once. Working moms perform this kind of mental jiujitsu all the time. I made a special trip to the House floor on June 23: I was eager to introduce my colleagues to my beautiful baby boy. Congresswoman Debbie Wasserman Schultz from Florida beelined right to me, along with Congresswoman Kathy Castor (also from Florida), Gabby Giffords, and many other women friends. The young male jocks of the freshman class welcomed me back warmly, too, though they weren't as practiced at greeting a colleague with an infant in her arms. Most said, "Good job!" and seemed proud as brothers nonetheless. While we chatted and voted—Congress can be surprisingly social—Henry fell asleep. Then I checked to make sure he hadn't exploded anywhere or spit up all over me and walked up the right aisle to the podium to address my peers. I'd asked Speaker Pelosi for one minute to speak, so I could thank my colleagues and the people of my district for their kind words and prayers. I also wanted to introduce Henry. The moment meant a tremendous amount to me personally, but I knew that it mattered symbolically. I was standing up before 434 of our nation's legislators sending a very clear message: "See? This is what a young mother in Congress looks like. I have a baby, who I will be caring for, and I will also be doing my job." What everybody says is true: The personal is political. I wanted my colleagues to take notice that I was going to represent my district and serve my country from the perspective of a new and working parent. I would view the world differently than most of my co-workers, and I felt very strongly that that difference was essential and good.

After the vote, Henry and I retreated to the Lindy Boggs Room, a suite off the rotunda reserved for women members of Congress. It has a bathroom, desks for making calls, a space for small meetings with female staff, and a nap room with blankets and threadbare chaise longues, including the couch that John Quincy Adams died on. The place is charming but not remotely fancy—imagine somebody's great-aunt's apartment, circa 1974. The Lindy Boggs Room became my new-mommy haven for nursing, pumping, showing off pictures, and receiving motherly and grandmotherly advice.

Susan, the woman who works there, was always thrilled to see Henry. Anytime he came with me to work, I'd stop in to see her and update her on life. Now that I'm a senator and no longer work on that side of the Capitol building, I see Susan less often, but she still keeps Henry's birth announcement, with that picture of Theo holding his baby brother, propped up on a small table in the entryway. Whenever I see it, my first thought is: "How sweet." My second thought is: "We need more pictures of congresswomen with their babies in here."

My life over the next few months was a bit unusual. At work, we were focused on getting out of Iraq without risking the safety of the troops. Democrats also wanted to pass an energy bill and a farm bill, and I wanted to preserve a safety net for dairy farmers, so they wouldn't lose their farms when the price for milk dropped below production costs. Because I was a freshman and essentially a nobody, I had no clout. Not even little Henry could get me a meeting with Senator Patrick Leahy, the small-dairy-farm champion from Vermont. So I crashed one of his fundraisers to hand him a draft of my bill. This was ridiculous, I now realize, as he knew the issue well and was already going to protect the farmers. But as a new mother and a new congressperson, I was a little too eager and earnest, and I was functioning on too little sleep.

Between votes, meetings, and committee hearings, I'd race to nurse Henry. During the first three months, he was home with my in-laws, and after that, in the House of Representatives daycare, about a half mile from my house. Our morning drop-offs there were not graceful: Jonathan and I arrived every morning bungling bags of diapers, wipes, fresh crib sheets, and bottles. Some days both boys were crying when we left them. But by the time I returned, they were always happy. Of course, I was only able to drop by to feed Henry because my whole world fell inside a one-mile radius. Without those quick nursing breaks, and the kindness and attention of the boys' caregivers, I could not have focused at work and done my job as well.

In the evenings, I skipped the cocktail-party networking–fundraising circuit that many members of the House thrive on when their families are home in their districts. Instead, most days, I picked up the boys from daycare at around 5:00 P.M. (If I had an end-of-day vote, Jonathan would do pickup.) Then we tried to eat dinner together at around 6:30 P.M., so we could play with the kids for a bit before heading into the vortex of baths, books, and bed. Just after the kids fell asleep, I'd go to sleep myself, so I could wake up to feed Henry every few hours around the clock. I know it sounds insane to a lot of people, but I didn't mind this. The house was quiet; Henry's crib was only a few feet away from my bed; and that silent third shift was our uninterrupted time. Even now, when Henry or Theo has an early-morning nightmare and sneaks into my room for a cuddle, I don't feel irritated. I'm grateful I'm there. I know that once the day starts and the boys are at school, there will be times when they need me and I'll be at the office or traveling. I do my best to be available to them when they need me. But this reality weighs on me, as it does every working mother: You can't be in two places at once.

Recently in America, we've fallen into a never-ending debate about whether women can "have it all." It's an absurd frame for many reasons. The first: For almost all mothers, earning money is a necessity, not a choice. Women work to provide for themselves and their children. We need to stop pretending that work is optional for all but the most financially secure American women.

Second: The word "have" in that phrase drives me crazy. It sounds like women are being greedy, trying to finagle more than their fair share, more than they're due. This is preposterous. Wanting or needing to have a job and a family is not like wanting a second slice of pie. Work and family are both basic tenets of our society. Every government should celebrate and protect both for all of its citizens. That we have come to a place where women seeking work *and* family can be seen as overreaching, even selfish, is inane.

Last: I hate the phrase "having it all," because it demeans women who *do* stay home with their children, by implying that their lives are less than full. One of the main goals of the feminist movement is that all women should be able to make the best choices for themselves and their families, and no one should be belittled, degraded, or disregarded because of what she chooses to do. Women's work needs to be valued fairly, by everybody, wherever it takes place.

So, please, let's stop talking about "having it all" and start talking about the very real challenges of "doing it all." The old debate pits women against one another and distracts the conversation from what truly matters—figuring out how working mothers can get the support they need to achieve economic security and build better, happier, more-balanced lives. We cannot keep talking about choosing to work as a decision women are making. Decades ago, when many of the workplace policies that still exist today were designed, America was very different. In 1960, only 11 percent of families with children under the age of eighteen relied on mothers as the sole or primary breadwinner. Today, it's 40 percent. Half of families today have dual-income parents. Only 20 percent have a father at work and a mother at home caring for the children.

We need to change the structure of our workplaces to reflect the face of our workforce. Too many of those in positions of power have no understanding of the issue. Too many can't imagine having to raise a family with few resources and no full-time caregiver at home. We must band together and hold legislators and business leaders accountable. Yes, we need to continue the fight to break the glass ceiling in every industry, but we also need to help women to climb up from America's sticky floor. Women make up nearly half of the workforce and earn more than half of the college and advanced degrees. Yet today's workplace policies do not reflect those realities. We are the only industrialized country in the world that doesn't offer some form of paid leave for the birth of a child or an illness in the family. Think about that—even Afghanistan and Pakistan do. Our refusal to acknowledge the change in America's workforce is undercutting our economy and our growth potential. All of us, especially women, need to fight harder and raise our voices louder. Every day that we don't, we leave more women behind, and our whole nation suffers.

Women ask me all the time how I manage work and family. I understand the interest, but as I always say, I'm not the issue. I have it easy compared to most parents. Serving in Congress gives me a level of flexibility that's exceedingly rare. I can work from home if I have an emergency. I can bring my children to work if I need to. (My staff can bring their children to work, too.) Henry has a box of markers in my office that he especially loves, and he relishes the rides on the Capitol's underground train system. Just yesterday, Theo had a fever and spent hours on my office couch, reading books and playing Minecraft. My day was more complicated, and I had to cancel a couple of meetings, but I managed.

Yet even with all the support I have and the flexibility my job provides, my life is not simple. For me, the biggest challenge is exhaustion. After an intense day of lobbying or negotiating with colleagues, often on emotionally charged issues, I go home and spend two or three hours taking caring of two growing boys—and for the last two years I've done this with my husband working in another city during the week. As tired as I am, after the boys go to sleep, I try to empty the dishwasher or fold some laundry, and if I can't wait another day, I sweep and spot-clean the floor where Henry's dinner landed instead of in his mouth. Still, I am thankful to my children for keeping me focused on what matters. If both boys claim that they're "staaaarving" when they get home, I take it as a challenge to make them something healthy within fifteen minutes that they'll actually eat: steak or turkey burgers, broccoli and carrots, maybe pasta or potatoes. About 90 percent of the time I succeed, and that simple victory feels good.

I fail more than I'd like to admit. Theo hates being late for baseball practice—and after 5:30 votes, he often is. Henry feels life deeply and can have a temper, and I don't always redirect it well. When he fires off insults—"You're the worst mommy ever!"—I attempt to state his feelings back to him so he can see that under his anger he's usually disappointed or frustrated. Sometimes this works; other times, it doesn't and he tries to kick me in the shins (tae kwon do–style, of course). At that point, do I scold the bad behavior or keep engaging on the feelings? These decisions don't feel intuitive to me. For advice, I call Erin (my parenting guru) or talk to Henry's teachers and the school counselor. It all helps, but still I feel like a failure for not knowing what the hell I'm doing myself.

The one task in my house that I truly hate is cleaning the bathrooms. I avoid it as long as I can, but with two young boys, the toilet area needs a lot of wiping up. (Aiming is apparently a learned skill, and Henry's not quite there yet.) Jonathan's favorite joke is a takeoff from the movie *Ghostbusters*, which the boys have seen. When the two boys are competing for who gets to go first, Jonathan says jokingly, "Don't cross the streams!" Naturally, this creates more mess and more kneeling on the bathroom floor with a Clorox wipe in hand. God gave me boys for a reason: They keep me humble.

Henry tends to be my household equivalent of the canary in the coal mine. Days before Jonathan is telling me that enough is enough and I should "do something about it"—meaning get my staff to pare down my crazy schedule—Henry gets clingy before he goes to bed. The more minutes of cuddling and mommy time he insists on right before sleep, the worse our family balancing act is.

Sundays when I am scheduled to work are the worst. One recent Sunday, when I was in the kitchen getting ready for a dreaded drive to the airport, I sighed.

"What's wrong, Mommy?" Henry asked.

"Oh, nothing, I just don't want to go to work today," I said.

Henry touched my hand and said, "Don't worry, Mommy. All mommies have to go to work." I nearly cried. I was so proud of my son for recognizing that work is part of who I am and that it's both necessary and good, if difficult at times.

But I mean it very sincerely: No one should worry about me. We should worry about the woman who cleans the office at night, or who puts in double shifts as an emergency-room nurse, or who works full-time for minimum wage and still lives in poverty. We should worry about women like Tiffany Kirk, who is struggling to raise her daughter while working as a bartender, earning $2.13 an hour, the tipped minimum wage. She works eight- to fourteen-hour days, and still she must rely on food subsidies and her local shelter. At times she shuts down her electricity or phone in order to save money for rent. But by far the worst trade-off Tiffany is forced to make is between enduring sexual harassment from patrons and earning less in tips. In her life, she says, she faces "many instances of being degraded by men—guys reaching across the bar and demeaning me because they know I depend on them to pay my bills. If I don't stroke their egos or play along, then they don't tip me, and that's literally taking food out of my daughter's hands."

These women don't want our pity, but they do need our advocacy and support. A year and a half ago, Laurie Greenstein's daughter, Leah, was in a terrible car accident and her legs were crushed. Laurie did not have any paid leave and could not afford to take unpaid time off, so she had to ask her elderly parents to care for Leah while she recovered. Amber Dixon faced a similar bitter trade-off: care for a child in need or put food on the table and a roof overhead?

Amber worked for nineteen years in well-paid industrial jobs because she wanted to create an economically stable life for herself and her son. But this came at a price. On Amber's first day in a new department for a local utility, she was told, "We never had a girl before," and "We don't go home for sick children here; that's why there are rescue squads and emergency rooms." Not long after, when at a remote jobsite, Amber received a radio message saying her son was sick at school. Given that she'd driven to the site in a truck with a group of co-workers, she had to wait five hours for someone to show up and give her a ride to her own car so she could take her son to the doctor.

Last year I also met Lucila Ramirez, who works as a janitor at Washington, D.C.'s Union Station. She is fifty-five years old and has held the same job for two decades, earning just above the minimum wage. Lucila gets no benefits: no sick leave, no days off. She's never been given a raise. Every day, Lucila moves closer to the date when she should be retiring, but that date keeps receding. Lucila can barely get by on $8.75 an hour. How is she supposed to save? If you earn federal minimum wage (state minimum wage can be higher) and work full-time, you earn $290 a week, or $15,000 a year. (If you earn state minimum wage, you likely earn about $350 a week, or $18,200 a year.) Think about that. How could you afford your rent or mortgage, decent food, medicine, and heat, let alone your kids' soccer shoes, a babysitter once in a while, on $15,000 or $18,200 a year? You couldn't. Sixty-two percent of minimum-wage earners are women, many of them single moms.

In May 2013, Lucila addressed some of my colleagues on Capitol Hill. Minimum-wage workers don't have lobbyists or powerful advocacy networks, nor do many of them have time to come to Washington and lobby for themselves, because they can't afford to take the time off. Few have much hope that their stories will make a difference. But when Lucila stepped up to the microphone in the Capitol, clearly nervous and dressed in her dark-blue Sunday best, the room fell silent. Lucila told the assembled she'd worked her whole life and felt fortunate to have a job, but nothing she did could pull her out of poverty. She lived in fear of growing old and infirm. Just before she finished speaking, she said directly to President Obama, with as much dignity as I've ever seen anybody summon, "You need to raise the minimum wage."

This would be good for everybody. Raising the minimum wage to $10.10 an hour would put more money in the hands of people who need it. Twenty-eight million Americans, including fifteen million women, would start spending more on food, clothes, and other basics. Economists estimate that $22 billion more would flow into the economy, and this would lead to more jobs. But these issues rarely gain traction in Congress, because too few of our representatives can relate. They don't earn the minimum wage. Most don't worry about childcare or family-sick-leave policy. The majority are male, well paid, and not the primary caregiver in their homes.

Imagine the choices a mother of two has to make, earning $15,000 a year, which is $3,000 below the poverty line. Does she buy her children healthy foods like fruits, vegetables, dairy, whole grains, and proteins? She probably can't afford to, and that alone kicks off a bad cycle. When children go hungry or eat less healthfully, their chances of learning well and reaching their full potential fall. Our economic policies are undermining our future. The promise of the American dream was that if you worked hard, you could make it into the middle class. If we don't raise the minimum wage, provide affordable daycare and universal pre-K, and mandate paid family medical leave and equal pay for equal work, we are allowing that dream to fade away.

———

When I was first elected to the House, I often picked up Theo at daycare at 5:00 P.M. and brought him to the Capitol. We'd enter the huge old building and hold hands as we walked up to the second floor on the marble staircase, the risers worn with age. In the House chamber, Theo could wander around as he pleased, and he loved it when we had a vote. To vote, members have two choices: One, approach the speaker's desk and hand in a small colored cardboard card—a red one for no, a green one for yes, or yellow for present, if you don't want to vote either yes or no. Or, two, place a small card similar to a hotel-room key in a machine with a slot on top and then push a button—red, green, or yellow. Most of the time, representatives choose the second, and Theo loved pressing the buttons. He'd jump at the chance to help me vote. After, he'd run around voting for anyone who would let him—most of the women and many of my male friends. He'd take the card and say, "Red or green?" Often, thinking he was pretty slick, he'd pretend to vote green when he'd been asked to vote red or the other way around. He always actually voted the right way, and we all watched to make sure he did, but it was very cute.

After voting, I'd buy Theo a hot dog or a peanut butter and jelly sandwich and an ice cream at the cloakroom snack bar. The cloakroom has a half dozen couches and comfortable chairs where members can talk or watch the news or a game between votes. Theo and I both adored those nights, and I think some of the older members did, too. Congress skews toward people in later middle age. Theo reminded them of their grandchildren.

Theo has made all kinds of guest appearances at my job. When he was about four, I hosted a political fundraiser and Christmas party at Hunan Dynasty and asked Senator Chuck Schumer to attend as my special guest. The event started at 6:00 P.M., so I collected Theo from daycare and brought him with me. (I no longer make the rookie mistake of scheduling my own events at such an awkward childcare pickup time.) Chuck loves kids and is not one to stand on ceremony, so when he arrived, he gave Theo a big hello and boosted him up on his shoulders. The gesture was very sweet, and it made me feel more comfortable that Theo was at the event—right up until the moment Chuck asked Theo if he'd like to use his new bully pulpit to address the crowd.

There were about thirty people, including advocates, friends, and other supporters, in the narrow private room. I didn't yet know Chuck very well. Did he understand that the extemporaneous speaking gig he was offering Theo might turn out very badly? I stood about three feet away, in case the talk went awry. My nerves were not calmed by seeing Theo play with Chuck's thinning hair. But I have to say: The boy did his mother proud. In his little jeans, sitting squarely atop Chuck's strong shoulders, he delivered a charming three-minute exposition on the importance of parents buying batteries before Christmas in case Santa brought gifts that required them. My tiny orator! I was beaming with pride.

Navigating the Senate with young kids has required more re-sourcefulness. When I was first appointed, I was asked to preside. That means sitting in the Senate chamber for a few hours while senators give speeches to a mostly empty room. It's an honor, in theory, but when no one is speaking, it becomes an unglamorous chore. The time slot I was given could not have been worse: 5:00 P.M. to 7:00 P.M. I tried to explain to the young male Senate staffer who issued my orders that these hours were impossible: I had an infant whom I needed to nurse during that time, and if I didn't feed him, I'd be extremely uncomfortable. (Any more detail than that would have fallen into the category of too much information.) The staffer didn't care. The Senate is an old institution, based on tradition and seniority, and as its most junior member, I was instructed to do as I was told, period. I tried to argue my side again, but the staffer wouldn't budge. So I took the issue on myself, making a list of junior senators and calling each to see if anybody would be willing to switch slots.

My Senate desk had once been Hillary Clinton's and before that Daniel Patrick Moynihan's. I'm pretty sure no one had ever made infant-scheduling calls from it. After a few no's, I reached Senator Mark Udall and I explained my predicament. He said, "Of course I'll take your slot!" We'd known each other briefly in the House, and I knew Mark sincerely cared about family and women's rights. He became my hero of presiding orders and my future partner in fighting for equality when we were working to repeal Don't Ask, Don't Tell.

My most recent hurdle has been figuring out what to do when a vote is called between 5:30 and 6:30 P.M. and I have the kids. (These days, Henry and Theo have to be picked up from school by 6:00 P.M., which means I need to leave work by 5:45 as most of our sitters are junior staff members from various House and Senate offices who work until 6:00 and can't start until 6:30.) Unlike in the House, children are not allowed on the Senate floor. For a while, during votes, I left the boys in Senator Harry Reid's office, a grand space accented with beautiful tiles, rugs, and fireplaces. I'd hand them my iPhone, say, "Don't move!," race twenty feet to the Senate floor, flag the attention of the clerk recording the votes, and race back. How much trouble could a four- and nine-year-old get into in thirty seconds? I didn't want to find out.

So I pressed for a better solution, proposing various rooms and spaces off the floor. The Senate has a cloakroom similar to the House's, except with no food. On the opposite side of the chamber, there is a formal room that is rarely used except by the teenage Senate pages, who like to study there. Both these rooms are enclosed and have couches where the kids could sit. But I was told we couldn't use them. Some of the senators raised concerns: What if the children were disruptive? What if other senators saw the precedent and began asking to bring in their grandkids? These worries struck me as theoretical, at best, given how few senators have young children and how rarely grandchildren visit during voting. (Read: never.) But we finally stumbled on a solution that was unexpected, simple, and, as it happened, a perfect metaphor for my life. The staff decided that I would be allowed to stand with my boys at the far Senate door and lean in my head to vote. Now I can hold my children's hands and do my job—what every working mother wants.

Chapter 6

Ambition Is Not a Dirty Word

It frustrates me how many people automatically assume the worst about ambitious women. You must be cold. You must be calculating. You must be arrogant and man-hating. This is a significant issue for women in politics. Too few people believe that you can be ambitious, feminine, and a decent person at the same time.

I was very disappointed when Hillary lost the presidential nomination in 2008. I believed in her so much that I was in denial for much of the campaign. I never lost hope, even when the electoral math didn't add up. I greatly admired President Obama's campaign, and from that first speech we all saw at the 2004 Democratic convention, I knew he could transcend the typical political rhetoric. But my commitment to Hillary was personal. Her words and experiences resonated with me. I was particularly affected by her descriptions of her mother's courage—how, at age eight, her mother was sent across the country with her sister to live with her father's parents. Six years after that, Hillary's mother left that unhappy home to work as a maid and build an independent life. I believed with all my heart that if the country really got to know Hillary, she would be our next president. But the push-back against her was harsh. Political hacks moaned about Hillary's age; toy Hillary nutcrackers appeared in airport gift shops.

The Hillary I knew was a brilliant, well-prepared, and strong leader, as well as a wonderful mother, daughter, and wife. Her depth was evident the day before the New Hampshire primary. In a cafe in Portsmouth, a sixty-four-year-old woman asked Hillary how she managed to keep going on the campaign trail. Hillary's answer was raw; her voice broke and she nearly cried. At last the world could see Hillary for who she was—a complex, emotional, even vulnerable person, not a cartoon ball-buster in a pantsuit, who wanted to rule the free world. Hillary's humanity added to the depth of her ability to serve. It seemed that some voters had a hard time seeing or believing that.

Secretary of state had not been Hillary's original goal, but I thought the president showed strength by appointing her. She'd be outstanding at the position, and President Obama's willingness to give Hillary power inside his administration was healing for the Democratic Party. Still, the appointment was a shock to me.

I was two years into my first term in Congress and had just wrapped up a grueling reelection campaign and a 24-point win against my opponent. Jonathan and I, needing to get away, decided to take his parents and our kids to Disney World. There I spent a few days lining up for rides like Space Mountain and evenings walking through Epcot Center, eating couscous and shish kabobs. Then, one night, as Jonathan and I were buying ice cream for Theo and my in-laws, my email in-box started to flood. Within seconds I understood why: Hillary had been nominated to be secretary of state, and various news sources had started listing my name as a possible replacement for her. I was dead last on every list, but my name was there nonetheless.

Questions started swirling in my head. I was still so new to my public-service career: I'd only been in Congress for two years. I'd just turned forty-two, which was young for a female politician, though not that young for a male. Joe Biden famously won his Senate seat at age twenty-nine and had to wait until his thirtieth birthday to be sworn in to meet the constitutional age requirement for the office. Was it too presumptuous to even think I was qualified to be a senator?

On the flip side, I believed in my training, drive, and common sense. Like many women of my generation, I'd grown up being told, "You can do anything you want to do if you put your mind to it." I was inclined to believe this, judging from my mother's and grandmother's examples. "A woman has got to be able to say, and not feel guilty, 'Who am I, and what do I want out of life?'" Betty Friedan wrote in *The Feminine Mystique* in 1963. "She mustn't feel selfish and neurotic if she wants goals of her own, outside of husband and children." My generation inherited these assurances. I played varsity sports, made partner at a law firm, ran for and won a seat in Congress. Having goals and the ambition to achieve them is part of who I am. To me, aiming high isn't egotistical or arrogant; it's vital.

But politics is often about more than leadership. It's also about paying your dues, and I certainly hadn't paid enough to be a United States senator yet. Carrying Henry around Disney World, I thought of my friend Nita Lowey, a dedicated and well-respected congresswoman from just north of New York City. Nita and her husband, Steve, had been assigned by the House leadership to mentor Jonathan and me when we first came to Washington. More important, she'd served for over two decades and political lore had it that she'd deferred running for Senate eight years prior when Hillary declared her intentions. As far as I was concerned, if Nita wanted to be senator, it was her turn. So before I let my brain focus in on Hillary's now-empty Senate seat and whether I might want to fill it, I called

Nita. While the boys splashed in the pool at the Beach Club hotel, I said, "Obviously Hillary was just named secretary of state, and before I even considered submitting my name, I wanted to speak to you."

"Oh, Kirsten, you're so kind to call. But I'm thinking I'll be able to do more if I just stay where I am," Nita said. During the eight years Hillary served in the Senate, Nita had gained a lot of seniority on the House Appropriations Committee. She was now the chairwoman of the Foreign Operations Subcommittee. She planned to stay put.

So I started having conversations with people I trusted, asking if they thought I should consider forwarding my name for Hillary's seat and, if I did, what advocating for the job would look like. I thought it was reasonable to submit my name, but I needed a reality check.

The process involved winning over just one person: Governor David Paterson. The New York Constitution charged the governor with appointing someone to fill the vacant seat for twenty-one months, until the next statewide election was held. I talked with my chief of staff, Jess Fassler, and then another three or four important friends and political advisors who knew the governor and New York politics well. But the more I talked to trusted confidants, the less crazy the possibility appeared. Why would I *not* seek the Senate seat? Sure, representing twenty million people as diverse as the citizens of New York State was daunting. But I'd entered public service to do something meaningful. Jonathan, always the most important voice, recognized that making a difference was the only metric that mattered.

Or at least Jonathan realized that having an impact was all that mattered once we started talking about the Senate seat in earnest. On our vacation, I downplayed the possibility. My mind tends to race far ahead; Jonathan prefers a more measured pace. So in Florida, I just told Jonathan that the Senate seat was looking like a vague possibility, as at the very least he deserved to know why I was spending so much time on the phone.

Back home, we began to discuss the job for real. Jonathan asked one question: "Can you help more people if you're in the Senate?"

I said, "Yes." I told him I'd be representing millions more people. Senators also have far more influence, regardless of seniority. I'd have to serve in the House for twenty more years to have as much opportunity to shape the debate as I'd have in the Senate on my first day.

That was the end of it, as far as Jonathan was concerned. He switched to wondering why I was doubting submitting my name at all. We were in this to help people. I could help more people in the Senate.

So I gathered up my courage and called Governor Paterson on his cellphone. When he didn't answer, I said to his voice mail, "I'm so honored to be considered for this; I would love to have the opportunity . . ."

Then I hung up, relieved. There. Done. That is, done until the next day, when I got a callback from his assistant, saying my message was inadequate. I had to state explicitly that I wanted to be considered, not just that I was *honored* to be considered. I called back and clarified: I wanted the job, and I hoped I would get it.

I already had a warm and positive relationship with the governor, as we had taken the time to get to know each other when it didn't matter. This is an essential part of my worldview: Be kind to others and build relationships most when no one is watching, because that is when you are your most honest and genuine self. Years earlier, in the summer of 2003, a friend had suggested that I meet David—who was then a state senator—just to talk and get to know each other, no ask on either end. We spoke one afternoon by phone when Jonathan and I were vacationing at the beach. After chatting for an hour, we made a date to meet later that summer in New York City. I was pregnant with Theo, and the day we planned to get together, a transformer broke down in the Midwest, causing a major blackout across the Northeast. New York City was in chaos. My office building was evacuated, and I assumed all plans were off, so I walked down the fifteen flights, my round belly preceding me, and made my way to my apartment on the Upper East Side. Paterson, worried because he knew I was pregnant, went to my office anyway, in case I needed a ride home. That kindness stuck with me. I figured I might have a shot.

While it's true that most females born after 1960 have been told from childhood, "The sky's the limit" and "You can be anything you want to be," a surprising number of women still hesitate when applying those mantras to their own careers. They need to be talked into believing in themselves and assured that others won't think less of them for setting high goals. For instance, when I first ran for Congress, I hired a terrific woman named Rain Henderson as my policy director. Typical lawyer that I was, I thought the first thing I needed was someone to do research and help me form considered views on issues like education reform and the Iraq War. Granted, in Campaigning 101, they tell you that the first person you have to hire is your finance director, and that chances are you'll never have enough money to hire a policy director at all. But I was running my own campaign at this stage, so I didn't care.

Before the election, Rain got a call from one of President Clinton's policy advisors, telling her that the Clinton Foundation was hiring staff for its childhood-obesity initiative. She was really excited about this and asked me for a meeting and some advice. We sat down in the lobby of a big D.C. hotel where I'd just attended a reception, and I asked Rain what the job would entail and for whom she would be working.

Rain said, "Oh, I'm not sure yet. I'm applying for the number-two job, and the number-one job is available, too, so I don't know who my boss would be."

I nearly exploded out of my seat. "What?! Why aren't you applying for the number-one job?"

Rain said, "I don't know if I'm qualified."

Mentoring moments crop up when you least expect them, and you have to seize the opportunity to be the right person to say the right thing at the right time. "Rain!" I said. "Are you kidding me? They're going to hire somebody who's not as smart as you, not as capable as you, probably a guy, and you're going to be kicking yourself every day because you'll know you could be doing a better job! You need to apply for the top spot."

Rain looked stunned. "You really think I should?"

"Of course you should! If you don't get the number-one job, which I know you will, then you can apply for the second job."

I made Rain promise that she'd apply for the top job, and she got it. She excelled beyond all expectations and today is running a new initiative called Clinton Health Matters, which develops programs around the country to reduce preventable disease.

I've learned a few things about ambition over the years, particularly in the months around my Senate appointment.

One: Do not fall for the lie that ambition is counter to femininity. What creature is stronger and more motivated than a mother protecting her children? Use that feminine strength. It's a huge asset.

Two: Trust yourself. If you don't, nobody will believe in you. Confidence is infectious and builds momentum. Share your faith in yourself. You'll be surprised how quickly others will come to have faith in you, too.

Three: Draw your own map. Yes, take advice and learn from others, but also embrace the fact that no two people have the exact same background, experience, talents, or goals. Create your own plan and stick to it. Uniqueness is a sign that you know yourself and your situation.

Shying away from ambition isn't just about a lack of self-confidence. In 2005, a group of professors at Georgetown University published a study that analyzed people's feelings about ambition and gender in politicians, surveying responses to candidates looking at just two contrasting pairs of traits: male or female, ambitious or not ambitious. And the results were stark. Respondents said they were less likely to vote for power-seeking women compared to power-seeking men and even non-power-seeking women. They perceived ambitious women as only out for themselves. They even reported ambitious women provoking feelings of disgust.

Few women are immune to this. Even the most powerful women in the world, consciously or not, tend to downplay their achievements and strengths. Oprah Winfrey once asked former secretary of state Condoleezza Rice, "You graduated from high school when you were fifteen. At what point did you know you were a very smart girl?"

Rice answered, "Never."

Oprah Winfrey herself, champion of self-empowerment and the wealthiest self-made woman in America, didn't do much better in owning her role in her astronomical financial success. "I don't think of myself as a businesswoman," she told *Fortune* magazine. Even Drew Gilpin Faust, the first female president of Harvard University, told *The New York Times,* when asked how she got her job: "Things sort of happened."

Psychiatrist and Weill Cornell Medical College professor Anna Fels, author of *Necessary Dreams: Ambition in Women's Changing Lives,* interviewed dozens of successful women for her book and found that none would admit to being ambitious—*none.* Everybody hated the term, believing it implied egotism, manipulation of others, and self-aggrandizement. Fels found two regular refrains: "It's not about me, it's the work," and "I hate to promote myself." Men don't trip over themselves in this way, nor does anybody question their sanity or sexuality for pursuing what they want.

Part of the problem, according to Fels, is a lack of clarity about what ambition means. Historically, she argues, "Women have confused it with narcissism, with people who simply want to promote themselves at any cost. But really, what ambition is about is getting appropriate recognition for your skills." Fels gravitated toward the study of ambition because she felt that her own ambition was socially unacceptable, even as a child. "When I was about seven, I had a notebook at school, and I would write poems and stories and illustrate them," she told an interviewer. "And I had this acronym that was like magic, like a secret pact with myself. I didn't even tell my sisters its meaning. It was IWBF—I Will Be Famous." Ultimately, our tangled views of ambition come down to word choice. Just as many women reject the word "feminist" but believe in opportunity and equality for all, many women reject the word "ambition" but believe in trying to achieve difficult goals.

I knew that convincing Governor Paterson I was the right person for the job would require belief in my own ambitions. It would also require stamina and a strong support network, as whoever filled Hillary's spot would have to run and win a special election less than two years later. The candidate would then have to turn around and run *again* for a general election two years after that in order to keep the Senate seat.

So when I interviewed with the governor, I told him, yes, I could handle the responsibilities of senator and I could also run two strong, back-to-back statewide campaigns. My support system was solid and national—I could raise the necessary funds. My second congressional campaign had been one of the most grueling and expensive in the country. The Republicans were determined to win back my seat, and my opponent was very wealthy and could fund the entire campaign. He spent $7 million; I raised and spent $5 million—and to raise $5 million for an upstate New York district is not easy or common. Few candidates have the desire or discipline to make dozens of calls every day, week after week, month after month. Frankly, it's a lot like learning Mandarin, which I did in college: endless hours at a desk. Difficult, intense, often tedious, and necessary.

I made just three other points to Governor Paterson: One, as a woman and a mother, I might see challenges and opportunities differently from the other contenders, but I could be a voice for all New Yorkers. Two, having been born and raised in upstate New York, and having lived in New York City for over a decade, I could represent the entire state. I knew the struggles facing farmers, manufacturers, and small businesses, and I knew I could do a good job. And three, I could run a winning campaign.

As I stood up to leave, the governor warmly shook my hand. "You know, through this process, I've heard the nastiest things about you! And you have reflected none of that. It makes me like you even more." Apparently, others had spent their interviews slamming possible opponents. After the interview, I quietly left Albany, as I didn't want to build up anyone's hopes, including mine. The only person who knew I was in town that day, besides my chief of staff, was my mom.

On Thursday, January 22, I started receiving calls from the governor's team, asking for follow-up information and details about where I stood on various issues. By the end of the day, I was told that a decision had not been made but that I needed to be in Albany the next day to stand behind the nominee, whoever that might be. I was excited I was still being considered and I figured it was probably down to just two. So I flew home, telling my family that I thought I had a good chance but that nothing was official yet.

At the Albany airport, a battalion of reporters greeted me, asking, "Why are you here? Are you going to be the new senator from New York?"

I tried to play it cool. "I don't know whether a decision has been made. I was asked to come to stand behind whoever was chosen, and so I'm here," I said. Inside, my mind was racing. I'd started letting myself think, "This just might happen. You never know. It could be me."

My chief of staff, Jess, and I spent the evening at my brother, Doug, and sister-in-law Liz's house. Doug cooked a pot of homemade chicken soup, which was exactly what I needed. I paced back and forth across their kitchen in my light-blue polar-bear pajamas. Every hour or so, a state leader and ally of the governor would phone to ascertain my views on another issue: gay rights, immigration reform, gun violence, and healthcare. At 2:30 A.M., Governor Paterson called. "Congratulations, Kirsten," he said, cutting to the crux. "You're the senator from New York."

I was elated and overwhelmed. I hugged Jess, Doug, and Liz and shouted something senatorial like, "Holy shit, can you believe it?!" Then I did what I always do at times of great stress: I took a deep breath and kicked into autopilot. My mind fixated on the next ten things I needed to do. Top of the list: Call Jonathan. I was giddy and asked him to come with the kids to Albany on the next flight from D.C. Next I called my parents. Then I started to figure out what to say in my speech the next day.

In the morning, fueled by adrenaline, I put on my nicest black suit, did my best blow-dry and makeup, and headed to the Capitol to meet my family, who had gathered there. (Jonathan thoughtfully waited until after the ceremony to tell me that their trip was a near disaster and they'd barely made their early-morning plane at Dulles.) My mom had already made sure the kids' clothes were presentable and Henry, then eight months, was fed. He just needed a quick diaper change, which we did on the governor's conference table. Two minutes later, Henry was much happier. In fact, he slept from the minute the ceremony started. More concerning was Theo. He wasn't feeling well and seemed to be running a fever. In his groggy state, he asked if he could stay by my side during the speech.

"Of course. Just sit right there next to the podium and rest," I said, deciding I needed to risk it.

Theo promised to be good, and he was. The only major glitch of the appointment ceremony was my too-long speech. Afterward, on my way to our car, I called the pediatrician to make an appointment for Theo. No party or champagne for the Gillibrands that day, just a doctor's visit and antibiotics.

The whole first six months on the job were like drinking from a fire hose. Outside my home district, few of my nearly twenty million new constituents knew me or liked me, and my job was to win their trust. I needed to keep my head down, my spirits up, and work hard, reaching out to people and listening to their concerns so I could understand them and work on their behalf.

Given that I'd been appointed and not elected, I hadn't had the chance to define myself, which my opponents and detractors started doing for me, often in harshly negative ways. I got called a parakeet with no original thoughts, a cipher, and Chuck Schumer's puppet. The *New York Observer* published a cartoon depicting me as gun-loving Annie Oakley. (My rural congressional district included a lot of hunters, and I support their rights.) *El Diario,* an influential New York City Hispanic newspaper, ran an unflattering picture of me, along with the headline ANTI-INMIGRANTE. I was nicknamed Tracy Flick, the aggressive, comical, and somewhat unhinged blond high school student played by Reese Witherspoon in the movie *Election.* I'd liked the film well enough, but this was not a compliment. It was a put-down to me and other ambitious women, meant to keep us in our place. Yes, I'm competitive. I fight for what I believe in, and I drive hard toward my goals. Does that make me ruthless or crazed? No.

Jonathan was my hero, always trying to bolster my spirits. "Ignore them. They don't know you," he'd tell me. But he hated it. As he had during my first campaign, he asked to stop receiving our daily email of press mentions. He couldn't handle it.

I tried to accept where we were and work to turn the situation around. I was new at my job, and I needed to address my inexperience and weaknesses head-on. My two most glaring issues were my House records on gun violence and immigration. Previously, I had only looked at these issues through the lens of my small, rural upstate district, which didn't suffer greatly from gun violence or families battling a broken immigration system to stay together. But these issues mattered intensely to parts of New York State.

Congresswoman Nydia Velázquez, an outstanding leader in the Hispanic community, was skeptical of me and openly shared her opinion that I was a poor choice to fill Hillary's Senate seat, because of my limited knowledge of immigration issues. So the day after I was appointed, I visited Nydia at her home in Brooklyn. I made it clear that I wanted her guidance in understanding what immigrant communities were going through, and over time and many frank conversations, we built a trust and rapport. By six months into my term we'd found solid footing. This meant a tremendous amount to me, and the photo from her endorsement of my 2010 Senate campaign still hangs in my office. Nydia also encouraged me to meet Sonia Sotomayor, and that resulted in Senator Schumer and me recommending her to President Obama to sit on the Supreme Court.

My then A rating from the NRA was another sticking point for critics. Until this point, I had never represented areas with prevalent gun and gang violence, and on the day I was sworn in to the Senate, the New York *Daily News* ran an article calling for me to meet with the family and friends of seventeen-year-old Nyasia Pryear-Yard.

Nyasia was an honors student from Nazareth Regional High School in Brooklyn, who'd recently been killed by a stray bullet from an illegal gun at a teen dance club. Her community was still in shock and mourning her death. Press reports said parents felt so scared and terrorized that many refused to let their own children outside at night, even to empty the garbage.

So, two weeks later, I visited the Nazareth students, who made a sign for me to read as I entered their school: IF THERE IS A BETTER SOLUTION, FIND IT. Nyasia's parents urged me to make their daughter's life mean something, to use their pain to prevent other children from dying. I gave them my word that I would fight, and I meant it. I committed myself to doing whatever I could to end gun violence in this country. My decision wasn't a calculated evolution, as some speculated, and it wasn't a political consideration. It was my clear answer to the intensity of Nyasia's parents' pain and the collective misery of her community. There was no other possible course.

I spoke with Ray Kelly, then New York City's police commissioner. He explained that eight out of ten guns used in crimes in New York City were trafficked from out of state and that 90 percent of those weapons were illegal. I met with New Yorkers Against Gun Violence and the Brady Campaign and heard their painful stories. I met with Representative Carolyn McCarthy, who ran for Congress after losing her husband to a shooting on the Long Island Railroad; she had worked tirelessly for years combating gun violence. Each meeting, and all the violent deaths retold, fueled my anger. That year I wrote and introduced my first bill on gun reform: legislation that would for the first time make gun trafficking a federal crime and give law enforcement the teeth required to shut down the so-called Iron Pipeline of trafficked weapons.

When the Senate refused to pass meaningful gun reform after the Sandy Hook tragedy, I was devastated, along with much of the nation. All those children and their teachers, every one somebody's beloved son or daughter—and my colleagues couldn't do anything.

To be a part of that was infuriating. Congress couldn't even pass simple commonsense reforms: to stop gun trafficking, require background checks, ban assault weapons, and limit the size of magazine clips. I wrote a bill, built bipartisan support for it, and was filibustered by two votes. Every time there is a school shooting, or a child is killed anywhere, I feel gutted and enraged. We need to keep fighting and speaking out until we create change. How can we stay silent when children continue to be shot? The more Americans that speak up and hold their representatives accountable, the closer we get to a safer and stronger nation. We must keep fighting—for Nyasia, for the students at Sandy Hook, for all of us.

I knew from the moment I changed Henry's diaper on Governor Paterson's conference room table that I was never going to be a typical senator, so I never tried to be. As Eleanor Roosevelt once said, "Do what you feel in your heart to be right—for you'll be criticized anyway." Voters began reaching out to me with their concerns in unconventional ways, so I reached right back across the same channels. I started working with women's magazines and mommy blogs, communicating through traditionally female means, talking not as a senator would to a voter but the way one mom would talk to another. This was unusual, but who cares? I was determined to be my own person—I strongly believe your individuality is your strength. As much as I admired Hillary, I knew I wasn't walking in her precise footsteps. She had to travel a harder road, leading a generation that didn't take women's rights for granted, as my generation did. Hillary and her peers made securing women's rights the fight of their lives. My generation has a responsibility to take the power and freedom they fought for and make the world a better, safer place.

Chapter 7

Now We're Yours

Along with Hillary's desk, I inherited some of her legislative agenda, including the task of passing a 9/11 healthcare bill.

If you're a normal person, you're probably thinking, "What's the problem? That sounds fine! What could be more galvanizing to the nation, and more clearly important to the Senate, than taking care of the brave first responders who got sick from helping others in the wake of a terrorist attack?"

But Washington is a strange place and, as we all know, things that should be easy can quickly become difficult. Hillary had been shepherding the 9/11 healthcare bill in the Senate. The House had held about twenty hearings on the subject. But still—zero progress. The bill had languished for nearly three years without a vote.

Yet I was optimistic. Anything's possible, right? On one of my first days in the Senate, Jess, my chief of staff, sat me down. He wanted me to define what kind of senator I wanted to be. I had a very clear answer already in my head. "I want to be a voice for the voiceless. I want to take on lost causes and issues with no champion." My mission might sound corny, but I was absolutely earnest. To this day I repeat those words all the time: "Be a voice for the voiceless." That's honestly what I want to do with my energy and time here. The 9/11 healthcare bill was right in my wheelhouse.

So I gathered my legislative staff and together we began strategizing about how to push the 9/11 healthcare bill through. I positioned my desk at an angle to the walls of my office, to make the room feel more friendly, but I was on a quest. I wanted to get this done.

After that first strategy meeting broke up, Jess walked into his adjoining office, then leaned his head back through our shared door. "You know there's no way to pass a 9/11 healthcare bill, right?" he said to me. "I mean, we can do all the things we've just agreed to do, but you're not actually going to win."

"What do you mean?!" I said. "We can't start fighting with the assumption we're going to fail. We have to believe we will succeed. *I* believe we will succeed. You really think that there's no way to pass it?"

Jess said, "Well, yeah."

The problem, he explained, was a lack of sympathy. Yes, the nation had come together in grief and patriotism in the wake of 9/11, but few on Capitol Hill wanted to help New Yorkers. People in the Senate viewed New York as a wealthy state (never mind the fact that New York has poverty levels similar to most other states'). They also viewed the bill as an entitlement program for New Yorkers, disregarding the reality that 9/11 first responders came from every state in the country. Each year, more men and women who'd worked and lived at Ground Zero were becoming ill and dying from toxins they'd inhaled. Yet the bill still didn't have enough support.

So, true to form, I flipped into operation mode and wrote a 10-point list.

1. Draft a bill.
2. Formally introduce the bill to the Senate.
3. Ask for a hearing on the bill.
4. Hold the hearing.
5. Build co-sponsors, including Republicans.
6. Build momentum to garner support.
7. Coordinate with the House members to make sure the changes I made to my bill from theirs are acceptable.
8. Find a way to pay for the proposed reform.
9. Find Republicans who will help build more support.
10. Hold the vote.

To further back down the naysayers, I ordered six copies of the self-help book *The Secret* and distributed them to my staffers, who, as I expected, responded by laughing at me and rolling their eyes. Almost everybody who worked in my office was young; some had staffed my first congressional campaign. My management philosophy has always been to build and train a good team from within, then trust your people. I always look for smart, hardworking, honest individuals and then give them freedom to do their jobs. But my legislative director, Brooke Jamison, is a pessimist by nature, and I wanted her, and everyone else in the office, to see the power of positive thinking. If we were going to be effective champions of lost causes, we needed, at the very least, to believe in ourselves. So at the risk of looking ridiculous (and let me assure you, I did. What kind of loony boss makes her staff read an intellectually suspect New Age-y self-help book?), I made everyone read *The Secret* and discuss it with me. The book is out there at times. It includes an example of wanting a new car and advises the reader to imagine sitting in the driver's seat, hands on the wheel, as if that will make the car materialize. But for me, optimism is essential. When I'm depressed and pissed off on the road, missing my kids and feeling like a loser, I try to flip my mood by asking my staff to tell me three things that they feel grateful for in their lives, and I always share my own. I also make myself positive-thinking reminders. During my 2010 election, for instance, I set a grandiose fundraising goal for the first quarter: $3 million. I knew this wasn't entirely realistic, but I believed it was crucial for my credibility in Washington. To keep my thoughts positive I changed my computer password to 3M1stQ. (You can laugh, but it worked.) A positive mindset sets a tone for my office. To this day, whenever I or one of my staffers starts spiraling into negative thinking, somebody will say "See the car!" or "Put your hands on the steering wheel!" It's a joke, but also important. Those phrases are our code for "Picture success."

At this time, my life outside the office, for a change, felt relatively under control. I knew I needed time and mental space to learn how to do my new job well, so Jonathan and I sprang for full-time help: first an au pair for a year, then my former nanny from New York, who came down and stayed with us Monday to Friday. We couldn't afford this for more than two years, but those months were a godsend. I can't tell you how huge a relief it was to know that if I had to work late or travel outside D.C., my children would still eat healthy meals, their clothes would be clean and folded, and my household wouldn't collapse.

In the years since then, I've learned how to handle the pressures of my job and caring for a young family. But that took a lot of trial and error, in part because there were almost no role models for women who had babies and were hands-on parents while holding elective office. To this day, young women approach me all the time with their real and, to my mind, very valid questions about whether they can serve and grow families at once. Will they have the energy? How would a daily schedule look? How will they piece together their entire lives?

When I was newly elected, my friend Debbie Wasserman Schultz, a congresswoman from Florida, was a terrific support to me. She understood what it felt like to juggle kids and constituents—to be dealing with permission slips, pink eye, baseball games, and national security, all at the same time. But her kids lived back in her home state. She was on the phone every night, navigating math homework, hearing about playground skirmishes, and deciding whether it was fair to have a bedtime of 7:30 P.M. when a sibling got to stay up until 8:00. Her struggles were just as hard, if not harder, than mine. But I couldn't look to her for logistical advice. What are you supposed to do when your babysitter cancels forty-five minutes before a vote? Or how to cope when you're about to do a national television interview and a teacher calls to say that your son doesn't feel well and says he can't breathe? (Answer: Drop everything and race to the school to find out he's had too many hits on his asthma inhaler. Then speed to the emergency room, trying not to hyperventilate yourself.)

In the early days, just figuring out how to schedule myself, let alone my children, was complicated. Even the basics got overlooked. My staff and I didn't set aside time for buying food, eating food, bathroom breaks, or traffic delays. We didn't factor in how tired I'd be by 8:00 P.M. in California if I'd woken up at 6:00 A.M. on the East Coast. When I was seven months pregnant with Henry, my finance director, Ross, planned a trip to California. When I read the itinerary on paper, I knew it was going to be a hard trip, but I thought I could just power through. For the record, I adore Ross. He's one of the most fun-loving, well-meaning people I know, and his warm smile and disheveled looks reel in affection. But he has a habit of doing what he wants to do and asking for forgiveness later. Given his appeal, this generally works. But on that California trip, his boyish "Sorry, boss" was not enough.

Day one in the Bay Area, we drove from San Francisco down to Silicon Valley, taking seven meetings back-to-back. I was exhausted. Every part of my pregnant body ached, so in the early evening, just before our last event, I asked if we could please stop by the hotel so I could rest for a minute, fix my makeup, and brush my teeth. The minute I entered my room, I crumpled. I was so tired, physically and emotionally, that I couldn't stop crying for ten minutes. I honestly didn't believe that I had the strength to pick myself up, put my game face back on, and head out the door. Fifteen minutes after I was supposed to have been downstairs at the car, Ross called me in my room.

Before he could say anything, I said, "I'm not coming down."

Ross said, "Kirsten, you have to come down."

I said, "Go fuck yourself." Very professional, I know.

At that moment, I hated Ross, I hated my job, and the last thing I wanted to do was make cocktail party conversation. A few minutes later, Jess, who'd been alerted by Ross, phoned me from D.C. He managed to talk me into washing my face, redoing my makeup and heading downstairs, but I was not happy about it. I felt so angry at my team for not looking out for me, and even angrier at myself for not better knowing my limits in terms of managing my time, health, and career. Women are notoriously bad at putting their own well-being first. I am definitely not the mother whose first instinct in an airplane emergency is to put on her own oxygen mask before helping her kids.

As soon as I entered Ross's car, I said bitterly, "I bet you didn't even think to ask if they have cats." I am extremely allergic to cats. Ross knew this. One of my office rules is that I need advance warning before walking into homes with cats, so I can take an antihistamine. Ross even has a sign to hang above his desk. Theo made it. It reads, NO CATS.

But Ross had not asked, and he started begging forgiveness. I was having none of it. The moment we entered the home, which was beautiful, I started sneezing. I summoned every ounce of energy left in my body to smile, chat, give a short speech, and answer everybody's questions amid all my nose-blowing. I'm amazed that I managed to stay on my feet.

Since then, I've learned how to schedule myself. I know my limits and how to keep from reaching a place of diminishing performance. I understand that I can get depleted not just by long hours on a given day but from the cumulative effect of long hours over weeks and months. Now my staff tracks the number of hours I work each day, how many days a week I go to the gym and have dinner with the kids, how many weeknights I attend events, and how many weekends a month I travel. These metrics, printed in capital letters at the top of my daily calendar, let me know how tough a day, week, or month will be overall. That trip to California was far too much. That night, I was asleep before my head hit the pillow.

In my early Senate days, I also needed to get a better grip on handling the press. I thought I was a pro at this, and I prided myself on my ability to put my thoughts into clear, articulate terms. But my experience with reporters had been as a congresswoman from a rural district. Now the journalists I encountered were more skeptical. If I was long-winded, they wouldn't stop me; they'd let me ramble into their tape recorders and nod along blankly. Worse, I was unguarded. One day I ate lunch in the Senate dining room with a reporter from a Long Island newspaper. I really liked him. We had a nice rapport and we talked for an hour about the financial collapse and various ideas for regulatory reform. When we stood up to say our goodbyes, he said nonchalantly, "You own guns, right?"

I said, "Yes."

"Where do you keep them?" he asked.

Without pausing to think why he was asking the question or whether I should answer it, I said, "Under the bed."

Huge mistake. Our exchange about guns became his whole story. It made the front page of *Newsday,* and that led to headlines across the state. I was so frustrated with myself for not answering more thoughtfully—and for answering at all. The topic was irrelevant to our interview. Besides, what was I thinking, telling the world, without any context, that I kept guns under my bed? One had been a raffle prize, the other a gift. Both were still locked up in their original cases. Neither Jonathan nor I had ever loaded either.

But along with outing some weaknesses, my first year in the Senate helped me rediscover some strengths. Those years of Bible study and teaching children in New York had been really grounding for me. I didn't talk much about my faith in the House. But during those hard first months in the Senate, I needed every resource I had, and that included my religion. When I was invited to the weekly Senate Prayer Breakfast to tell my story about how God fit into my life, I said yes.

A lot of people didn't know the religious side of me—top among them, Glen Caplin, my beloved and straight-shooting New York communications director. His response to learning about my years of Bible study? "That's effing weird, but okay!"

I loved speaking at the Senate prayer breakfast. Over coffee in a conference room under the Capitol dome, I talked about finding my way from corporate law into public service and the parable of the talents. For those who don't know it, the parable of the talents is a story from the New Testament about a landowner who gives money to each of three servants before he leaves on a long trip. Two use the money wisely—they double their wealth and are rewarded for it. The third buries the coins in the ground, gains nothing, and is punished. "God gives us certain things that we're supposed to use to help others," I said to my new colleagues. "As a lawyer in New York, I wasn't using my talents. I knew I could be a great advocate and work to serve others and that I needed to make a change in my life to use those God-given qualities for the greater good. That's what I want to do with my life and this opportunity now that I'm in the Senate. I want to be a voice for the voiceless. I want to take on lost causes."

That prayer breakfast was such a great joy for me. It felt so good to connect the old and new parts of my life. From that point on, whenever I was asked to speak in a church, I tried to say yes.

In October 2009, Reverend Calvin Butts invited me to the Abyssinian Baptist Church in Harlem. I was very nervous before the service. On the surface, I didn't seem to have much in common with many parishioners, and I wasn't sure how pleased they'd be to see me. But the reverend welcomed me with such warmth and grace that, the minute I walked into the sanctuary, I crossed out much of my prepared speech and decided to speak extemporaneously from the heart.

I told the assembled that I'd promised myself that as long as I had the honor of representing New York, I was going to use my seat to amplify the voices of those who needed it most. Then I started talking about Scripture from the Book of Ruth. "You know the story," I said. "It was a time of famine in Bethlehem. Naomi and her family moved to Moab for a better opportunity. But when they arrived, terrible things happened. Her husband was killed. Then both of her sons were killed. Naomi was left with nothing." Naomi decided to return to Bethlehem—she had nothing to stay for. She begged her two daughters-in-law, Orpah and Ruth, to start their lives over, somewhere hopeful and new. Orpah did, but Ruth refused. She returned with Naomi to Bethlehem and took on Naomi's burdens as her own.

I started channeling my inner pastor, who is unexpectedly close to the surface, quoting Scripture. " 'Where you go I will go, and where you stay I will stay,' " I said. A part of me comes alive when speaking to a church crowd. " 'Your people will be my people, and your God my God.' And just as Ruth said to Naomi, I make the

Erastus Corning 2nd and Polly Noonan (front row, first and
second from right), in group at Assembly, circa 1937.

My parents' senior prom, spring 1958.

Mom, holding Doug, at her
law school graduation, May 1966.

Dad didn't call me
Loudmouth for nothing.

On the porch at our Putnam Street house.

Doug, Erin, and me (left). Erin and I are wearing dresses sewn by our mother.

Erin and me (right) in tutus in front of our *Brady Bunch*–style house in Albany.

Cousins and friends in Grandma's backyard. I'm in blue. Dad is holding a fish he caught in her pond.

In the kitchen of the Albany house. Polly is holding my cousin Joseph.

Around age nine in my immaculate Type A bedroom.

My First Communion, May 1974.

Erin (right) and me at our first charitable event, the Gold and Silver Ball at the Grand Hyatt Hotel, benefitting the Youth Counseling League, New York City, 1983. My job was to solicit ads and raise funds.

With my friend Elsa Scagel (left) at Emma Willard School graduation, 1984.

The Dartmouth squash team—I'm in the front row, third from right. Coach Aggie Kurtz is standing at far right.

Connie Britton and
me in China.

With my Dartmouth
senior-year roommates
Regina Glocker (left)
and Reghan Foster Diaz.
Our other roommate,
Elizabeth Keenan Thompson,
took the photo!

With Kathy Baird (left) and Erin hosting a holiday party
in Erin's and my first New York City apartment
(at 86th Street and Second Avenue).

At a Hillary Rodham Clinton fundraiser at Felice Axelrod's apartment,
where I first offered to work on her Senate campaign,
New York City, 1999.

Jonathan and me when we were first dating.
Elaine Bartley's wedding, Lake George,
New York, September 1999.

With Mom and Grandma, 2001.

My ladies' bridal luncheon at the Lotos Club, with my New York crew, New York City, April 6, 2001. From left to right: Angela Burgess, me, Marianne Fogarty, Lucy Fato, Gillian Eastwood.

At my bridal luncheon. From left to right: my sister-in-law Elizabeth Rutnik, Paige Crable DeMarco, Jennifer Whalen, me, Elaine Bartley.

Our wedding day, Yale Club, New York City,
April 7, 2001.

With baby Theo.

Theo and Jonathan
painting signs for
my 2006 campaign.

With Bill Clinton and Congressman Mike McNulty
the day before Election Day 2006.

A full crowd at my congressional swearing-in, Speakers Lobby, Capitol. Left to right: Doug with children Alexandra and Douglas, Erin with children Matea and Massimo, Dad, me, and Theo, Jonathan, cousin Cathleen Montimurro, Mom.

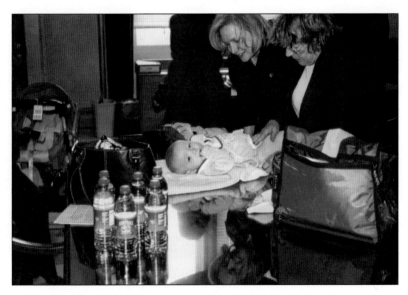

With Mom, changing Henry's diaper on Governor Paterson's conference table, January 2009.

Theo's seventh birthday, November 2010, the morning
after I won the Senate special election.

Rachel Zarghami Wolf with son Kyle, me with three-year-old
birthday boy Henry, Elaine Bartley, Caroline Caputo,
and Jennifer Whalen (front), May 2011.

With Connie Britton and her adopted son, Eyob, January 2012.

With Gabby Giffords and Debbie Wasserman Schultz on the day
Gabby threw out the ceremonial first pitch at the annual
Congressional Women's Softball Game, June 18, 2014.

(PHOTO BY JEFF MALET, MALETPHOTO.COM)

Greeting President Barack Obama following the memorial service
"Together We Thrive: Tucson and America" at McKale Memorial Center,
the University of Arizona in Tucson, January 12, 2011.

With Dad on Election Night 2012.

With Jonathan, Henry, and Theo on Election Night 2012.
(PHOTO BY NANCY BOROWICK)

My swearing-in with
Vice President Joe Biden,
Henry, and Theo, old
Senate chambers,
January 2013.

Walking back to my in-laws' home in London (behind us is a statue of Saint Thomas More), Christmas Day 2013. Both boys were well behaved in church for Granny and Papa.

same statement to you. I will stand with you. As long as I have the honor of representing New York, that will be my mission. With faith and unity, no challenge is too great that we cannot overcome it together."

I heard a few people shout, "Amen!" and "Preach!"

When the reverend took the pulpit again, he had a wide grin. "A lot of politicians come to this church," he said, "but they don't all know the Word."

About a year later, Al Sharpton invited me to his House of Justice, also in Harlem. It was the first place I went after being appointed, and this time it happened to be the reverend's birthday. I had a great morning. Not only did the reverend welcome me back with open arms, the assembled really got behind me. The applause rose as I compared the reverend to Joshua, and President Obama and other contemporary leaders to the Joshua generation. God's instruction to Joshua was that, in order to win the battle over his enemies, he needed to rally all the voices of his people. Together they could shout down the walls of Jericho. "So let's shout down those walls of injustice," I said, my voice escalating. "Shout down those walls of lack of opportunity. Shout down those walls of degradation that our communities struggle with."

When I finished, Sharpton bellowed, "Reverend Kirsten Gillibrand!"

The most significant fight in my life against injustice and degradation was the battle to repeal Don't Ask, Don't Tell. A few months into my first term, Kathy Baird, my old law-firm friend, asked if I would talk with one of her legal clients: a young man named Dan Choi, who had been kicked out of the military for violating Don't Ask, Don't Tell.

Dan was everything you'd want in a soldier. The son of a Korean

American Baptist minister, raised in Southern California, he decided to serve in the military after seeing the movie *Saving Private Ryan*. He liked the idea of dedicating his life to serving a higher cause. After high school, he enrolled in West Point and graduated in 2003 with degrees in Arabic and environmental engineering. In 2006, he began serving in Iraq as an infantry officer in the U.S. Army's 10th Mountain Division.

Dan loved the military and its stated values. But over time, Don't Ask, Don't Tell made his life feel untenable. He'd known he was gay when he enrolled at West Point, but he thought he could hide it. Then he fell in love—and you know how that is. Love is important and consuming. He didn't want or believe he should have to keep his relationship secret.

"I thought the military would be a place of character, integrity, and honor, and I put everything into it," Dan told me as we sat at a long wooden table in one of the beautiful tiled rooms just off the Senate floor. "But because I'm gay, I had to lie about who I am to everyone I care about." When a group of gay and lesbian West Point graduates organized to fight for the repeal of Don't Ask, Don't Tell, Dan joined their effort and offered to be their spokesperson. As such, he appeared on *The Rachel Maddow Show* and came out on national TV. That automatically ended his military career.

Now Dan didn't want others to suffer in the same way he had, and as we sat together in our heavy wooden chairs, he asked for my help. Keep in mind that this was in 2009, before the national debate about gay marriage and its legalization in many states had begun. The public and my colleagues were far less comfortable with gay and lesbian rights than they are now. But fighting for justice on civil-rights issues like this was the reason I'd chosen public service. I told Dan I would wholeheartedly advocate for him and the repeal of Don't Ask, Don't Tell.

Given my newly minted Senator status, I had to research where my colleagues stood on the issue. The primary person focused on the repeal was Senator Ted Kennedy, and, sadly, he had brain cancer and was very ill. I assumed someone must be carrying Kennedy's work forward, but I learned this was not the case.

Arguments against the Don't Ask, Don't Tell policy could be found everywhere. In addition to being morally outrageous and corrosive, Don't Ask, Don't Tell undermined military readiness. Since 1994, when the law was first implemented, approximately thirteen thousand well-trained military personnel had been discharged from the U.S. military for being gay. More than two thousand of those people were experts in mission-critical disciplines. The military lost close to 10 percent of its foreign-language speakers. The cost of implementing the policy, from 1994 to 2003—including recruitment, retraining, and separation travel—was somewhere between $190 million and $360 million. I didn't understand how a reasonable person could think that such money would not have been much better spent on equipment, mental or physical health services . . . almost anything.

Moreover, the policy was counterproductive, and its enforcement was based on a lie. In discharge letters given to soldiers like Dan, authorities claimed gay soldiers "negatively affect good order and discipline" within their units. This was untrue. Opinion polls taken of military personnel stated that when soldiers were aware of their co-workers' homosexuality, as opposed to when homosexuality was hidden, it had *less* impact on their service. Even high-ranking military leaders agreed. In November 2007, twenty-eight retired generals and admirals urged Congress to repeal Don't Ask, Don't Tell, pointing out that over sixty-five thousand gay men and women were then serving in the armed forces and that over a million veterans were gay. Our military was then engaged in two wars abroad—Iraq and Afghanistan. Why would we choose to do anything to weaken our military's strength?

But as I began talking to my colleagues about repealing Don't Ask, Don't Tell, I felt reassured: Far more supported a repeal than one might have guessed. Senator Carl Levin, chairman of the Senate Armed Services Committee, was encouraging from our first conversation and agreed to hold the first hearing in sixteen years on the policy. Majority Leader Harry Reid also supported repeal and urged the White House and Pentagon to act. Republican women—Senators Susan Collins, Olympia Snowe, and Lisa Murkowski—all backed repeal, as well. President Obama mentioned repealing Don't Ask, Don't Tell in his State of the Union address.

For many people my age or younger, repealing the Don't Ask, Don't Tell policy was an obvious and urgent cause. Most of us wanted to fight for gay rights because we'd never considered doing otherwise. I loved Jonathan's brother, Simon, and his now-husband, Justo, and as a young lawyer, I was very close with some of the gay men at the office. Along with my single girlfriends—including Kathy, who introduced me to Dan Choi—we often worked late nights together, rolling our eyes and laughing when our straight married male counterparts would walk out of their offices at 6:00 P.M. saying, "I have to get home or my wife will kill me!"

But before too long I hit a major roadblock in my fight to get Don't Ask, Don't Tell repealed: The White House did not want me to introduce the bill. They wanted someone more senior to be in charge and responsible for passing it, someone on the Armed Services Committee, someone perceived as more conservative—specifically, Joe Lieberman. He had gravitas from years in the Senate; plus, he was an independent who could arguably bring in more Republican votes.

At first, I was disappointed. I had a bill drafted, I knew I could build support, and this was exactly the kind of work I wanted to be doing. I hoped to get started right away. But the reality was that White House support was a huge asset. If I cared about getting the policy repealed more than I cared about being in charge or getting credit, I had to acquiesce. So my mission became to convince Joe to take a strong lead. I spoke to him every other week for almost three months. Once he agreed, support cascaded. Susan Collins announced that she would be the lead Republican. I worked alongside everybody else, amplifying people's efforts, starting an online story project, and doing anything else I could to build momentum.

One Republican I was never able to convince was John McCain, though not for lack of trying. In November 2010, just after the election, Senators McCain and Lieberman invited me to join them and Senator Lindsey Graham on a congressional delegation trip to Afghanistan, Israel, and Pakistan. The point of the trip was to meet the troops and gain understanding of the war and regional security issues. My side project was to win McCain over to our side on Don't Ask, Don't Tell. McCain's wife had recently released a video supporting the repeal, so I figured we had a shot.

Visiting troops with McCain was like traveling with Bruce Springsteen. Everyone wanted a picture; supporters lined up to shake his hand. I knew if McCain joined our side, we'd be golden, so in quiet moments, I tried gently floating arguments like how great it would be for him to return from this trip and announce his support for gay troops.

He laughed, in a lighthearted way.

I tried direct tactics, too: "John, if you come out for repeal, then it's done. You're the maverick, you're the leader, you're the one people respect when it comes to military issues. Why not?"

Neither Joe nor I managed to change his mind.

A second roadblock came back home, on December 9, 2010, my forty-fourth birthday. Majority Leader Reid had promised us a vote on Don't Ask, Don't Tell repeal by the end of that Congress. But when that date rolled around, the Republicans had gridlocked the Congress, filibustering all legislation and blocking all votes, until they had the vote they wanted on taxes. I felt crushed and extremely worried. This meant we had to go back to Harry Reid and ask for another vote the following week. The hoops inside hoops that you have to jump through in the Senate can be maddening. What if there wasn't time for another vote before the end of the congressional session? That was my worst birthday ever.

Carl Levin, Susan Collins, Mark Udall, Joe Lieberman, and I all huddled off the Senate floor. We decided to introduce the repeal again as a stand-alone bill and call the vote up or down. This was a dicey move, but we were close to the sixty votes required, and we needed a moment of truth. Harry was our champion, and he gave us the second vote.

The next week, standing in the well of the Senate, I watched the votes come in. Eight Republicans supported us—our three Republican stalwart women plus Mark Kirk, Scott Brown, George Voinovich, Mike Ensign, and Richard Burr. We won, and I was ecstatic. I have the vote count sheet from that day framed and resting on my mantel. I knew that moment would have a profound impact on civil rights for millions of Americans and would propel forward our future fights for equality.

At the same time that I was working to repeal Don't Ask, Don't Tell, I was fighting to get the 9/11 healthcare bill passed. Throughout my first year in the Senate, men and women who'd been first responders at the World Trade Center had been coming to Washington to tell their stories. Many should have been in the primes of their lives, but instead they were sick and burdened with oxygen tanks and painful limps.

One of the first men I met was Ken George, a New Jersey firefighter who was dispatched to Ground Zero, or "the pile," as he called it, at 6:00 P.M. on September 11, 2001. His story was searing. As he walked down to the rescue site from Canal Street through the thick, burned-smelling air, a man handed him a photograph of a young woman and said, "I hope you can find my daughter. She's in one of the buildings." Not knowing quite how to respond, Ken put the picture of the young woman inside his helmet for safekeeping and said he'd do his best. Then he walked a few more yards, until another terrified person held out another picture of a missing loved one. Ken put the photograph in his helmet, too, and said again that he'd do his best. As the minutes passed, Ken began to notice pictures of missing people everywhere—on lampposts, mailboxes, sides of buildings. By the time he reached Ground Zero, he was already thinking, "My God, where do I begin?" Then he began his work on the search-and-rescue team, sifting through the pile that used to be the World Trade Center for remains. He never found a whole person, just body parts. Each time he found a body part, he raised his hand, and a police officer from the canine unit walked over with a dog. The dog sniffed the area for other remains. The officer put the body parts in a bag and took them away.

On that first night of search and rescue, while Ken and a team of policemen and firefighters were moving debris, green smoke started coming out of the pile. Ken began coughing uncontrollably and fell to his knees, as did the men around him. He got a terrible headache, then his airways got constricted and he could barely breathe. Nobody knew what the green smoke was—maybe Freon? Still, Ken kept working sixteen to eighteen hours a day in a job so dangerous that, during his first week, his superiors gave him a backpack filled with food and water to last a few days, in case the pile became unstable and trapped him inside. They also gave him a face mask, but the air was so thick with soot and debris that it clogged after a few hours. He tried to shake it out, but it was so hard to breathe in the mask while shoveling through rubble on hands and knees that he and the other first responders just took them off. As Ken worked, his eyes burned. Ash fell through the air like snow.

When I met Ken in 2009, he still suffered from PTSD. He'd had a heart attack four years prior, at age forty-two. "Can you imagine us turning around and saying on September eleventh, 'We're not going into the pile'?" he asked rhetorically, sitting across my desk from me in my office. Of course not. "They just told us to go out there, and we all did the best we could. Honest to God, I did the best I could as a person." Ken performed a horrible, solemn, necessary duty for our country, and our country was stiffing him on medical care.

John Feal didn't get sick after September 11; he got hurt. John, a construction demolition expert, worked as part of the cleanup and recovery effort, and on September 17, roughly eight thousand pounds of steel landed on his foot. John spent ten days in Bellevue Hospital, where he developed gangrene. Then he spent ten weeks in North Shore University Hospital, on Long Island, where he continued to fight the gangrene and lost half his foot. Over the next five years, John had multiple surgeries on both of his feet, and four doctors diagnosed him with PTSD.

In 2007, tired of being sick, John donated a kidney to a complete stranger. He also started becoming known in the first-responder community as the guy to talk to if you were sick. He attended all the workers' compensation meetings, Social Security hearings, and trials of his colleagues who sued the city to get benefits for injuries or illnesses they suffered from in the aftermath of 9/11. To help others more formally, he started the FealGood Foundation, dedicated to assisting first responders and other individuals injured physically or mentally as a direct result of their rescue, recovery, and cleanup efforts at Ground Zero. "There was more than frustration," he says of his community's experience. "There was disappointment and desperation. You name it, it was there." But he found fighting for his fellow responders healing. "I have yet to take a pill for my post-traumatic stress disorder," he recently told me. "Running my foundation and helping people is my therapy."

John is about as humble a man as I've ever known. "Listen, I'm never the smartest man in the room," he said with excessive self-deprecation the first time we met. "I have a high school education, military background, and then construction." But he was street-smart and had a natural instinct for how Washington worked. Long before the 9/11 healthcare bill landed on my desk, he'd been walking the halls of Congress, meeting with people, trying to get them behind his cause. Over time, he and I developed a slow, steady rapport. I knew he liked that I looked him in the eye when we spoke and that I insisted we call each other by our first names, even though he made fun of me for it. One time I called him on the phone and said, "Hey, John, it's Kirsten."

He said, "Kirsten who?"

I said, "Kirsten Gillibrand."

He said, "Senator, when you call, you have to introduce yourself! You just say Kirsten, then I don't think you're a senator. I just think, 'Who the hell is this?'"

But I still wasn't doing a good enough job for him.

I realized this for the first time in June 2009, right after I held a press conference on the issue with Senator Chuck Schumer, Congresswoman Carolyn Maloney, and Congressmen Jerry Nadler and Peter King, among other elected officials. During that conference I swore to the public that I'd never stop fighting, because of our country's "undeniable moral obligation to provide the healthcare and treatment these men and women deserve." Afterward, John turned to me and said, "Now we're yours."

Now we're yours. I felt humbled, inspired, and, I have to admit, intimidated. My commitment to the cause was rock solid, but many others, Jess among them, had been so skeptical about my ability to get anything done. So far I had my 10-point list, and I was working my way down it. I'd asked Senator Tom Harkin for a hearing (number 3). We'd held the hearing (number 4), though nobody besides

Harkin and me attended. Now Feal was putting his fate, and the fate of his fellow responders, in my hands. I had to do better.

One afternoon, in the Senate chamber, I asked Senator Patty Murray if she had time to chat. I can always count on her for excellent advice. So I told her what was going on, how I was flailing.

"How do I convince our colleagues to care?" I asked. "They seem to think it's only about New York."

Patty understood the problem and directed me to Senator Mary Landrieu. Mary had been very successful advocating for families in New Orleans in the wake of Hurricane Katrina. She'd made a national issue out of one that many in Congress would have preferred to keep local. That's what I needed to do now.

So the next day on the Senate floor, I approached Mary. Her advice was brilliant. "No one is going to care about New York if you don't tell them why they should care," she said. "You have to explain to people why this is horrible and why it affects them, too."

This was such a simple, effective way of thinking about advocacy. You have to impact people's hearts and minds. I knew that I hadn't done this yet. Yes, I cared about John Feal and the others, but I hadn't made it my mission to explain to others why they should care, too. I hadn't been emotionally persuasive. Here I was, holding all of their frustrations, fears, suffering, and anger, and then failing to broadcast those feelings to the world.

Toward the end of 2010, Congress entered a lame-duck session (the window of time between the election and the new term starting). I knew that if I ever hoped to pass a 9/11 healthcare bill, this was my only chance. If we waited until after the Christmas break, the new Congress would be in session and the Republicans would control the House. So, armed with Mary's advice, I began an intensive push to help people understand why they should care about the first responders. My mission was to tell the stories—their narratives of heroism, sacrifice, ongoing suffering, even death. I wanted my colleagues to feel the weight of what the Senate's indifference was doing to them. We'd called these people to serve, they'd become sick from toxins encountered in the line of duty—and we were refusing to care.

Heeding Mary's lesson, in the weeks leading up to the holiday break, we displayed in one of the Senate office buildings the badges of New York City Police Department officers who had worked at Ground Zero and later died from 9/11-related illnesses. Twenty-nine badges in all. The average age of the men who died was forty-six. So many young families destroyed, young families just like mine.

In my final push, I gave a speech on the Senate floor.

"I wish to make it crystal clear what this bill is about," I said to my colleagues. "This bill is about our first responders. This bill is about our heroes and their families." I spoke about Joseph Picurro, a steelworker, who for twenty-eight days helped cut beams in the pile in order to clear debris and find survivors. Years later, he was diagnosed with sarcoidosis, an inflammatory disease that affects the lungs and other organs. He had seizures, blackouts, and constant joint pain. He died at age thirty-four, in October 2010, leaving behind a wife and daughter.

I also read a letter written by Robert Helmke, a police officer who worked at Ground Zero after the attacks. Shortly after his time there, he was diagnosed with colorectal cancer. " 'Talk about crushing news,' " I read from his letter. " 'My wife and I sat in the car and cried as I asked her, "What did I ever do to deserve this?" ' "

At this point, I nearly lost my composure in a way I never had before as a public servant. Just as with the line *Now we're yours,* the question *What did I ever do to deserve this?* really got to me. I had to pause to keep my breathing even and hold back my tears. I really didn't want to cry on the Senate floor; that seemed like a total breach in decorum. I contained it, sort of, and continued reading.

" 'On July 11, 2006, I had major surgery to remove two tumorous parts from my small colon and have radiation on the large tumor in my liver. Before my surgery, I had four chemotherapy treatments and was in an emergency room three times to be treated for dehydration before finally having to go on an all liquid diet and intravenous feeding. I have a wife, Greta, and two young children, Garrett and Amelia, who have seen my health worsen since participating in the World Trade Center recovery. My favorite things in life are slowly being taken away from me—my work, food, helping others, and caring for my family.' " Officer Helmke died in 2007.

"These are the stories that tell us what this bill is about," I concluded in my own words. "Men and women who are suffering, men and women who have died because they did the right thing. What message are we sending here from this esteemed body if we cannot help those who came to our rescue, who were there to find survivors, who were there to find remains, who were there to do the cleanup when our government asked them to help?"

I left the podium feeling pretty insecure. Mary had given me great advice about why I needed to explain to people why they should care. But to show so much emotion? It seemed like stepping over the line.

Then a Senate page, a high school student, approached me and said, "Thank you so much; that was such a powerful speech." No one had done this to me before, nor has anyone since. Then another staffer walked up. "I've worked here for a long time, and that was the best speech I have ever heard." To be clear: I did nothing brilliant. I didn't deliver my address with great oratorical style. I didn't even speak in my own words. I just read a letter and allowed myself to feel the pain contained in it and show that pain to the world.

In my mind, that will always be the moment I learned my most powerful lesson about advocacy. I'd spent a long time making very little progress, but with Mary's advice I learned how to make a difference, and my confidence grew. Just as with Don't Ask, Don't

Tell, shortly before Congress adjourned for the holiday, we won our vote to provide healthcare for first responders and community members around Ground Zero. During the vote, John Feal sat in my office. He'd come down to D.C. with three buses full of men, women, and families. They spent the last few days walking the Senate office halls, saying to any senator they could find, "This is your last chance to be an American!"

Feal told me that he broke down and cried when he heard the good news. The bill passed unanimously. I'll be forever indebted to him for trusting me with his fight before I had yet to find my own way. We're all shaped by the challenges we work through. Those fights for justice and basic fairness taught me the single most important lesson in politics: To be an effective voice for the voiceless, you have to speak and fight from your heart.

Chapter 8

"You Need to Be Beautiful Again," and Other Unwanted Advice

Weight has always been an issue for me. I find this frustrating because I don't like being judged on my looks and, frankly, I'd like to spend less time thinking about my appearance, but there it is. I suspect the same is true for nearly every woman in America, especially those in the public eye. People—voters, clients, co-workers, everybody—will give you a limited amount of time and attention. Do you really want them focused on your hair, waistline, or shoes?

We may wish the world were different, and I truly hope it is someday, but we aren't there yet. So, until then, let's be realistic. As Daphne Merkin wrote about Hillary Clinton in *The New York Times*, "So shoot me: at the end of the day (and the beginning, if it comes to that), in the high-definition show business of politics—as in everything else—looks matter."

I'm sure you have a story. Here's mine:

When I was a girl, I was super-athletic and didn't spend a minute worrying about how much I weighed or what I ate. I just wanted to be fast, flexible, and capable on the soccer field, tennis court, or ski slope. In high school, I took up running with my dad. I especially loved our annual Thanksgiving jogs: We had short talks about nothing in particular, and the exercise made the day feel healthy.

The end of my dieting innocence came right before my high school graduation, when I went on a five-day liquid fast. (Nobody called a diet a "cleanse" back then.) Some of my girlfriends had come up with the plan in order to look as thin as possible for all our graduation pictures, so I followed along, stupidly. I had never restricted my food intake before and had a positive body image going in, but the fast planted a sliver of doubt in me. Plus, I was drawn to the challenge of it. Did I really have the willpower to forgo eating solid food for five days?

The first day I was starving. The second I was exhausted, dragging through my ninety-minute tennis practice. On the third through fifth days, I did feel a certain clarity about life, and determination filled my thoughts, but I felt no monklike purity. Sitting at our kitchen table, lying to my mother by saying I'd already eaten dinner at school, felt horrible. I knew she wouldn't approve of my fast (or my lying), but I didn't want to be told no.

I lost ten pounds in those five days, which I felt very virtuous about, until I gained it all back the following week. I can't say I looked any different in my graduation dress, and in the end I had made a bad bargain. With that fast, I stopped eating according to common sense and began buying into the idea that if I looked hard enough, I could find a magic formula that would make me thinner.

In college, I stayed focused on sports and didn't think twice about ordering a pizza at 11:00 P.M. to fuel late-night studying. I did see a nutritionist once during freshman year, because I was determined not to gain the "freshman fifteen." But I played sports two or three hours a day, so I really had nothing to worry about.

My dad loved coming to my games. He made it to most of my tennis matches in high school, and he followed my squash matches through college. He also noticed my insecurities about my weight and zeroed in on them. If we were out to dinner, he would say, "Don't eat the bread." When I'd call home on Sunday nights from Dartmouth, he'd ask some version of the same three questions: "How's school?" "How's squash [or some other extracurricular activity]?" "How's your weight?" I would blow off that last question with a simple "Great." I didn't like the scrutiny, but, looking back, I can see that I invited it in a way. I recently read all the letters I sent home from my sophomore summer in China, and interspersed between chronicles of hiking along the Great Wall and drinking toad venom as a remedy for food poisoning, I mentioned at least twice that I was losing weight. I even announced that while visiting a professor's home for a special dinner, I tried his scale and learned I'd lost eight or nine pounds. "I'm sure it's broken, but still—can you believe it?" I wrote. "Soy Bean Milk—the New Way to Diet—maybe I'll write a book someday."

No wonder he asked.

For law school, I moved from the mountain town of Hanover, New Hampshire, to car-crazy, body-obsessed Los Angeles, where I started spending all my free time running the four-mile loop around the UCLA campus and playing tennis with whomever I could find. I weighed only 125 pounds (ultimately my ideal "wedding weight"), but I wanted to be thinner—just five pounds would be enough. This was clearly desirable, or at least that's what Los Angeles culture led me to believe, because whenever I opened up a section of the *Los Angeles Times*, I'd see ads for gyms, plastic surgery, and diet plans. I wish I could say that I was self-aware enough to have resisted the message, but I was very impressionable. Instead, I tried the then-fashionable approach of eating a nonfat diet, which worked somewhat but didn't get my weight down to where I wanted it to be. Next, my roommate and I both signed up for a packaged diet meal plan, which also worked a bit but was too gross to stick with for long. So I went back to basics and refocused on being athletic.

Decades of research show that girls who participate in sports have higher self-esteem, less depression, more pride in their physical and social selves, and better health. A 2013 study from Ernst & Young even found that 67 percent of women in executive positions participated in sports as working adults. I knew athletics were central to my self-confidence and comfort with my body, but I was still susceptible to outside opinions. One evening, as I was slow-dancing with a boyfriend at a wedding, he said, "Is that your stomach?" Ouch. That was a blow to my ego and the death knell for our four-year relationship. At the time I was studying for the bar exam, running four miles a day, and he was making cracks about my belly (which, even at my tiniest, I've always had)? I was embarrassed. Then I was pissed. How could someone who supposedly loved me say something so superficial and mean? What was he going to say when I was pregnant, old, or fat?

A couple of years later, as a young associate, I went on a very strict diet: just vegetables, small amounts of fruit, no refined carbs, a little lean protein. I also didn't eat until I was hungry, which was at 2:00 P.M., due to all the coffee and diet soda I was consuming back then. Not the healthiest plan, but it worked ridiculously well. I lost twenty pounds over several months and had to take all my clothes in at least two sizes.

One night around that time, a few partners took a dozen or so associates, including me, out to an elegant dinner. We all needed the reward and acknowledgment for the grueling hours we'd been working. But when one of the partners rose and started speaking about my contributions, he spent all of thirty seconds praising my hard work and three times as long discussing my new haircut and how great I looked. Make no mistake: I appreciate a compliment as much as the next person, and if he had told me privately, I wouldn't have cared. But in front of my colleagues I felt undermined, thinking, "After all that work, you're talking about my hair—are you kidding me?!" I'd applied all of my intellect to that case, worked day and night, put in tons of travel, canceled vacations. Now, instead of recognizing my leadership, smarts, or dedication, he was praising my appearance. This would never have happened to a man. No partner would have raised her glass and said, "Wow, Joe, you must be working out really hard. Looking good!"

That night at the dinner, everyone laughed, and all the women exchanged knowing glances. We'd all been there at one time. I was uncomfortable and peeved, but I brushed it off. Everyone in that room knew me and my work well, so my reputation wouldn't suffer. But had there been strangers or new colleagues present, I would have been concerned. Comments about appearance belittle women professionally. Sadly, that's the culture we still live in. We need to start trying to change it by calling out undercutting remarks and educating our peers, but we also have to find a way to navigate the current reality. It's a tricky balance. Having more women in leadership roles will certainly help. Back in my twenties and early thirties, I didn't know how to deal with it.

Around the time of that disconcerting work dinner, I met Jonathan. I had a great fitness routine going through our courtship, eating well plus running and lifting weights. But after I settled into married life, I was happier than I'd been in years, which for me translated into going out to dinner and drinking a bit more. I've always loved good food. My favorite nights out with Jonathan are still spent at a French bistro consuming steak, salad, and red wine. So before we tried to start a family, I decided, once again, that I should lose a few pounds. I cut out carbs, and the weight came off without a big hassle; three months later I was trim and pregnant. But we all know how this one goes: I was thirty-six years old and I'd messed up my metabolism. I gained a pound or two a week while carrying Theo, seventy in all.

I was considering running for Congress during that pregnancy, so I spent a lot of time meeting new people to discuss my prospects, build relationships, and help other candidates. I think I shocked a few new acquaintances by being so large and pregnant, but I didn't really care. I felt only slightly more self-conscious after Theo was born. Sure, I was thirty pounds heavier than I was pre-pregnancy, but I looked like someone who'd just recently had a baby—no shame in that. I was also consumed with trying to figure out how to handle being a mom while pushing forward into a political career. I had no spare energy to stress about my weight. I was just like any new mother: overwhelmed and absolutely certain I was never going to be in *Vogue*.

But I was in for a rude awakening. A year and a half after Theo was born, when I decided to run for Congress, my looks, which I still wasn't thinking much about, became fodder for attack. Good, bad, ugly—it didn't matter. On the one hand, my opponent referred to me as "Just a pretty face!" And on the other, he used in his mailers the ugliest photographs he could find and even tinted my face green. In one picture he used from an outdoor press conference, my hair is blowing wildly, my expression is angry. Combined with the witchy skin tone, I presented the perfect embodiment of what many people fear: the crazed, power-hungry woman. I let this roll off me, certain that it would backfire, and it did. But it made me realize that in politics, beautiful and ugly are two sides of the same coin. People will use appearance to take women down, and they'll direct their message toward the positive or the negative depending on what's most expedient. A poll sponsored by Name It. Change It., a project of the Women's Media Center and She Should Run, found that all kinds of comments on female candidates' appearance hurt what voters think of them.

In 2007, during my first term in Congress, Jonathan and I decided we wanted to have a second baby. It took a fight for us to get that out into the open, but once there, the desire to build a larger family trumped everything else in our lives, so I didn't pause to question what it would be like to be pregnant in office, as the answer wasn't going to impact our plans. Besides, there was almost nobody to ask. Only five women had been pregnant in Congress before.

This time around, being pregnant was more complicated. I had been pre-gestational diabetic with Theo, and my doctor was concerned that I could be pre-diabetic again, so I preemptively went on a low-glycemic diet (no refined sugars, always consuming proteins with complex carbs at the same time) and started exercising every day. This was fantastic, as I'd lost touch with the tennis, soccer, and squash player in me and I hadn't run regularly in years. For the first time as a working mother, I blocked out exercise time on my schedule and instructed my team to protect it. What a revelation! Granted, this was easy to implement and stick with, because I viewed taking care of my body while pregnant as protecting the health and well-being of my child. Before then, something always came first: a meeting, a phone call, anything related to family. I had a hard time saying no.

Adding to the fun of blowing up in the public eye, the women's congressional gym happened to be closed for renovations, so I had to work out in the men's. Poor Congressman Collin Peterson was writing the farm bill that season, and not a day passed when someone wasn't standing by him in a sweat-damp shirt, bending his ear. As for me over on the elliptical: Many of my older male colleagues didn't know what to say but still felt compelled to offer advice, such as this gem: "Good thing you're working out, because you wouldn't want to get porky!" Thanks, asshole.

Wherever I went, my male colleagues seemed to comment. I couldn't ride an elevator in the Capitol without hearing, "Oh, my God, are you going to explode? Are you going to have that baby right now?!" The House chambers weren't much better. I had my private Shangri-La in the Lindy Boggs Room, but in the cloakroom, where I'd taken Theo for hot dogs, I couldn't even eat the only cookie I'd allowed myself all month without hearing, "You shouldn't eat that." Each night I'd regale Jonathan with something new. The prize comment came from a Southern congressman who said, as he held my arm, walking me down the center aisle of the House chamber, "You know, Kirsten, you're even pretty when you're fat." I believed his intentions were sweet, even if he was being an idiot. I wanted to put out a bulletin saying, "Please keep your thoughts about my pregnant body to yourself."

After Henry was born, my sacred gym time vaporized in a cloud of obligations. I barely had time to get dressed and dry my hair. Then, on December 1, 2008, as I strolled through Disney World with my family, Hillary was appointed secretary of state, and my whole life kicked into yet a higher gear. I was sworn in on January 26, 2009. Having never lost all the baby weight from Theo and now carrying more from Henry, I set out, larger than I'd ever been in my non-pregnant life, to meet the entire state. Along the way, I received an education in what New Yorkers thought of plus-sized me. One day I met with a labor leader to get his advice on how best to introduce myself to the unions and win their support in the special election I'd have to win a year and a half later. He said, "When I first met you in 2006, you were beautiful—a breath of fresh air. To win this election, you need to be beautiful again." I nearly choked.

It took every bit of my self-control not to react visibly. I wanted to tell the guy to go screw himself, then leave the table and go home and cry. Instead, I changed the subject to something neutral, like what meetings I needed to set up with which leaders. But after his comment, I was barely listening. Later, Jess, who'd been with me, asked if I was okay. I told him I was fine, but the truth is that I wasn't. I was worn down and depressed by the superficiality of it all, the endless discussions of what I looked like instead of what I thought.

Still, that wasn't the end of it. A month or so later I went out to dinner in New York City with a close friend who is savvy in politics.

He tried to speak gingerly. "So . . ." he said, clearly reluctant to say what he was about to say. "How would you feel if your picture was on the front page of the *New York Post* looking like this?"

I lost it right there, launching into a tirade of expletives that would have made my grandmother proud. "Fuck you. Fuck you. You're a fucking asshole. You go and have two children."

"Oooookkaaay," he said. I stormed off. We never spoke of it again.

Hillary Clinton, who has experienced this for so many years, has reached a point where she's risen above it. She recently defined herself on her Twitter bio as: "Wife, mom, lawyer, women & kids advocate, FLOAR, FLOTUS, US Senator, SecState, author, dog owner, hair icon, pantsuit aficionado, glass ceiling cracker, TBD . . ." In May 2012, she told Jill Dougherty of CNN, "I feel so relieved to be at the stage I'm at in my life right now, Jill, because if I want to wear my glasses, I'm wearing my glasses. If I want to pull my hair back, I'm pulling my hair back. And at some point it's just not something that deserves a whole lot of time and attention, and if others want to worry about it, I'll let them do the worrying for a change."

Listening to her has been a great help to me, as I imagine it has been to most female candidates. She has perspective on what we're all going through, what she calls "the kind of almost schizophrenia you live in when you put yourself out there." During a 2014 lecture at UCLA, she told a story about walking into a political meeting in Texas in 1972. "I had to walk down a center aisle and make my pitch about registering voters. Literally, out of my right ear I hear, 'I really hate that dress she is wearing.' And out of my left ear, I hear, 'I like that dress she is wearing.'" Retelling the story, Hillary sounded at peace and self-aware. When I was first appointed to the Senate, I wasn't there yet. The political operator's and labor leader's comments stung, in part because I knew I was too heavy for my own health. At that point, I wanted to be precisely where I was in my life—great job, supportive husband, two kids. But I had let my physical self go. I was fifty pounds heavier than I was before I had children. That was enough.

Thankfully, around that time, my college roommate Elizabeth Thompson suggested that I start playing sports again. I bought a new tennis racquet, a new squash racquet, and new workout clothes, and I found tennis and squash coaches, figuring that investing a little would help make my resolve stick. I also got my daily workout back on my work calendar, in figurative indelible ink, telling my staff that the first hour of every day after I dropped my kids at school had to be for exercise, no debate about it. This turned out to be good for everybody. Exercise made me a more effective worker, a nicer boss, a calmer mom, and a happier spouse. I also hired a nutritionist and began to write down everything I ate. My health started moving in a positive direction again.

Still, within a few months, I had the worst looks-related stumble I'd had in years. Sonia Sotomayor was to be confirmed by the Senate Judiciary Committee, and I was going to introduce her. This was a major milestone for women, Latinos, and the Court, and I was especially delighted because I'd recommended Sonia to Senator Schumer and the president even before Justice David Souter's seat opened up.

Until that point, I'd been an orthodox adherent to the professional rules about how to dress. From first through fourth grades, I wore my Catholic school uniform (blue jumper, white blouse, navy blue sweater, navy blue or white socks, and navy blue shoes). At fifth grade, the uniform switched to a plaid skirt with the same blouse, sweater, socks, and shoes. My sister fought with my mom about wanting to alter her uniform and take inches off her hemline, but not me. As a lawyer, I erred on the side of safety again in nicely tailored but conservative suits. As a politician, I followed all the rules I'd learned in campaign-training school, right down to no dangly earrings and nothing too shiny or complicated for TV appearances. (They wig out the camera.) I'm a person who doesn't mind a uniform. As I see it, if people are talking about your clothes, hair, makeup, or body, they are not talking about your ideas, message, or priorities. Remember the news coverage anytime Hillary's hair looked different or she wore something unexpected? No one reported on a word she said.

A few months before Sonia's confirmation, I went shopping at Macy's. Normally, as you know, I'm a black, gray, or navy suit kind of person. Crazy for me is a royal blue. That day, I'd given myself only forty-five minutes to shop, and I had about ten left when I stumbled on some fancy suits, brightly colored and feminine, the kind you might wear to a wedding. They looked so pretty on the rack that I didn't even try them on. I just found my size (16) and bought four—turquoise, green silk, pink with silver thread, and a cream-and-gold brocade. My mom and the ladies of upstate New York loved them, thrilled by the bright hues. "Finally! You're wearing some color!" they said. "They bring out your eyes."

On the morning of the Sotomayor confirmation, I met up with President Obama and accompanied him to New York for a speech he was giving to celebrate the hundredth anniversary of the NAACP. I wore a black suit—big surprise. (Actually, I made extra sure to wear black that day because black photographs well on me, and I was hoping for a picture of me with President Obama getting off Marine One, his helicopter.) This was the first time I'd traveled with the president. We talked about his speech and how historic it was for him. He asked me about my family.

After landing back in D.C., I wanted to change into something celebratory for the confirmation hearing, so I ran home and put on one of my new special-occasion suits, the cream-and-gold brocade. Then I rushed over to the Senate chambers for the swearing-in, where I sat at a table next to Sonia, who was looking very stately and refined in her blue suit. The moment I started to introduce her and the cameras began snapping, I knew I'd made a serious wardrobe mistake. The white flashes were glinting off the brocade. I felt as sparkly and out of place as a Christmas tree in May. Who could possibly have paid any attention to my words? *The New York Times* confirmed this, posting on their blog, The Caucus, "Senator Kirsten Gillibrand, clad in a satin brocade suit that practically casts a glare around her on television . . ."

I'd broken my number-one rule: Wear nothing that distracts.

Through that whole year, I stayed committed to losing weight, and much to my surprise, reporters started asking to interview me about it. The first was Michael Saul, from the New York *Daily News.* He called my office and sheepishly asked Glen whether he thought I would consider doing an interview for a diet story.

Glen's response? "No way am I going to ask her that. Are you out of your mind?" Clearly he'd heard from my House communications director about the time an Albany newspaper requested to photograph me while pregnant. "I am not Britney Spears," I snapped. "I'm not showing everyone my baby bump!"

But then Glen and I thought about what it would mean to discuss my diet and exercise with the public, and realized I should say yes to the request. Eating right and maintaining a healthy weight are nearly universal struggles for Americans. I wanted to connect with people, not hold myself apart. Why not tell my story?

Opening up that way did not come naturally to me. As a lawyer, I'd been trained to leave the personal aside. (I was used to giving long answers to questions, another habit I needed to change.) But being a public servant is different. People want and deserve to know who represents them, and the more I embraced the conversation about diet, health, and fitness, the more comfortable I became with it. Talking about weight loss, like talking about baseball or parenting, builds a simple bridge. Hey, I have fat jeans, too! People want to know that you share their struggles and goals.

Still, the first interview I did as a dieting mom made me extremely nervous. I was talking with Dana Bash from CNN while sitting on a park bench in front of Theo's school, with Henry on my lap. I worried that people would take me less seriously if they knew I kept a food log or had trouble resisting the kids' mac and cheese. But I was having such a hard time with the press in those early Senate days that I decided all-out honesty couldn't hurt. My hope that I'd reach more women offset my fears of humiliation and rejection.

It's strange how it all worked out: I'd always wanted voters to know that I'm a tenacious person, and what finally convinced them was that I'd possessed the determination to lose fifty pounds. From then on, if a women's magazine wanted to run a story focusing on my diet strategies, fine with me. A subset of voters seemed to genuinely care that I ate fruits, vegetables, whole grains, and lean meats and fish, aiming for roughly 1,200 calories a day. They wanted to know that I ate carbs in the morning, in the form of whole-wheat toast or oatmeal; grilled chicken and steamed vegetables for lunch; low-fat cheese or nonfat plain Greek yogurt and a piece of fruit in the afternoon; then back to lean protein plus vegetables for dinner. Very boring and trivial, I realize. But losing weight, as many of you probably know, is tedious and dull. I exercised four or five times a week, typically in the mornings before work, lifting weights, running, or, even better, playing tennis or squash, sometimes with Al Franken (who is as charming and funny as a senator from Minnesota as he was on *Saturday Night Live*). The only time I majorly strayed from my diet was the pizza and beer I consumed with the congressional women's softball team after we finally won a game. *Capital New York* ran stories like KIRSTEN GILLIBRAND DIET REVEALED!, showcasing the glory of a new mother fitting into her Levi's red-tab jeans.

I'm sure many of my colleagues thought airing this side of my life was preposterous or unprofessional, but I didn't. Being a public servant is being a connector. I want to meet people where they're at, which is often at the dinner table. When I argue childhood-nutrition policy in the Senate chambers, the issue for me is not abstract. Besides, the public was right: The same part of me that had the willpower to resist liquids besides water and decaf coffee—not to mention the hard candies and mini chocolate bars hidden in the desk drawer at the corner of the Senate chamber—really did translate into not giving up on our 9/11 first responders. Persistence is persistence, at home and at work.

After losing that fifty pounds, I was back to the other side of the coin: receiving comments about my appearance for looking better than I had in years. One of my favorite older members of the Senate walked up behind me, squeezed my waist, and said, "Don't lose too much weight now. I like my girls chubby!" He meant well, but those words didn't go over as he planned.

Women are sometimes concerned that if they are too blond or too curvy, some people may assume they are not substantive. (How many blonde jokes have you heard?) This is a legitimate worry. As Anne Kornblut writes in her excellent 2009 book, *Notes from the Cracked Ceiling*, Sarah Palin's "good looks were problematic in their own right, drawing attention that could be superficially seen as positive but was really a liability in political terms. . . . What did it mean, politically, that men wanted to sleep with Palin? Did that kind of thing draw any votes, or was it a sheer insult? Could Caribou Barbie, as she was called, be taken seriously as a vice presidential candidate?" According to Kornblut, during the 2008 presidential campaign, men Googled "Sarah Palin naked" and "Sarah Palin bikini" in droves.

Men don't seem to face the same problem. Male actors, like Ronald Reagan or Arnold Schwarzenegger, segue into politics just fine. Not so for female actors—at least not yet. The one relevant exception to this theorem is Jennifer Granholm. She was a model before she ran for governor of Michigan in 2003, and for her campaign, she shot her ads in ways that obscured her beauty—in safety glasses at a manufacturing facility, in black and white. She wanted to be respected and listened to; she feared her looks would interfere with that.

At the end of my year of weight loss, I met with Anna Wintour, the formidable editor in chief of *Vogue*. I knew she was very smart, savvy, and a political heavy-hitter, so I asked for the meeting to hear her thoughts and advice about the fashion industry in New York. Before our breakfast together, I did quite a lot of fretting over what she'd think of my black Elie Tahari dress and jacket. But during our coffee, I came to understand that Anna doesn't just produce an aspirational magazine with sometimes-bewildering clothes. She marshals a $10-billion fashion industry, a huge economic engine for New York and our country.

That day, we talked about trade, environmental, and manufacturing issues facing the garment industry and how clothes production and design impacted the state. By halfway through our meeting, I'd developed an enormous respect for Anna. She's tough and thoughtful behind those sunglasses, and I'm a woman who loves tough and thoughtful women, especially when those women support other women. By the end of our meeting, we'd discussed getting together to play tennis sometime. Anna gave me a list of things she thought I should do. One was to meet with four or five designers and retailers who could help me understand the finer points of the fashion industry. Another was to allow her to run an article and photograph of my family and me in *Vogue*, to introduce myself and some of the issues I cared about to her readers.

Given my love of lists, I set about checking off everything Anna had suggested right away. The more industry leaders I got to know, the more my perspective on the fashion business changed. This was not a frivolous community. Many of the women involved were very active politically and making a real difference in many people's lives. Diane von Furstenberg, Donna Karan, Nanette Lepore, Eileen Fisher, and Tory Burch all focused on issues such as international women's development, healthcare, earthquake recovery in Haiti, New York City manufacturing, mentoring organizations for at-risk youth, and micro-lending to women-owned businesses. The only time I felt out of my element in Anna's world was when I entered the *Vogue* fashion closet. I'd gone to the magazine's office in Times Square to decide in advance what to wear for the photo shoot. There I found rows and rows of shoes and bags I could never afford and the most beautiful dresses and jackets I'd ever seen. While I was being fitted in various ensembles by Anna's personal tailor, Glen, Jess, and I all stared at one another. This was very far from my home turf. I felt like I'd walked through the looking glass.

The *Vogue* shoot and interviews turned out to be terrific experiences. I knew that the glossy photos of me in designer attire might distract from my message, but I felt it was a risk worth taking if it allowed me to reach a wider audience, especially young professional women. If I could inspire a few to become more involved politically—to run for their towns' school boards, or advocate for special-needs children, or organize their neighborhoods for safer streets—the effort would be worth it to me.

Appearance and how much to think about it is a never-ending question in most women's minds. I haven't put it to rest myself, not by a long shot. But I've learned that how I look and feel is important to me, for reasons beyond health and vanity. It may sound clichéd, but it's true: If I look and feel good, I'm more positive and more confident. If I'm confident, people are more likely to listen to me. If more people are listening, I have more power to fight effectively for what I believe in.

I've also learned that most issues about appearance can be resolved by zeroing in on one's goals. My primary goal is to serve well. I don't want how I look to detract or distract from my advocacy.

Perhaps someday this conversation won't be necessary. I certainly hope so. As Daphne Merkin wrote, "We study our female politicians as closely and obsessively as we do in part because they still remain something of an anomaly."

Until that changes—and I hope it's soon—I'm going to keep it simple. If I have to wear a navy blue suit to work every day to be heard without distraction, so be it.

Chapter 9

Be Kind

Two days after Hurricane Sandy, as I was driving through the wreckage on Staten Island, I came upon a New York Police Department SCUBA team searching for the bodies of two missing boys, Brendan and Connor Moore, ages two and four. During the storm, the power went out in their home. Glenda Moore, the boys' mother, spoke to her husband, who was working for the city that night, and together they decided it would be safest at a relative's house in Brooklyn. So Glenda loaded the boys into their Ford Explorer, buckled them in their car seats, and started driving. But the storm was still gathering force, and the rain was falling hard and fast. Within a few blocks, the car flooded and stalled.

Glenda sat behind the steering wheel for a minute, trying to figure out what to do. Staying in the stalled car and waiting to be swept away seemed like madness. So she unbuckled her boys, grabbed their hands, and began to walk with them to higher ground. As she was walking with her sons, a ten-foot storm-surge wave rose out of the Atlantic, flooding the street and moving with such force that it ripped the boys from Glenda's arms. In a panic, she climbed a fence and rushed from house to house, frantically looking for Brendan and Connor or anyone who could help find them. Eventually she spent the night on the porch of an empty home.

Two days later, when I passed through, the Ford Explorer was right were she'd left it. All around were crushed trees, broken boats, and devastated homes. Staten Island was despairing. The two boys had died.

About twenty minutes after seeing the SCUBA squad, I met up with Senator Chuck Schumer and a half dozen other local elected officials about a mile away from the search area for the boys. We were meeting to assess the damage. None of us was prepared for how bad it was. When I joined Chuck, I could barely focus. Those boys weren't all that much younger than Henry and Theo. I kept thinking about the mother, trying to find a perspective from which her loss seemed survivable.

As we walked the streets after our press conference, I was torn from my thoughts by the sound of a woman screaming just behind me, to my right. When I turned around, I saw her walking very quickly, racing to catch our group. She was yelling with such panic that I couldn't understand what she was saying until she was just six or seven feet away. Then I heard her clearly. "I'm dying! I'm dying here and no one is doing anything!" she screamed.

I had seen the aftermath of Hurricane Irene and Tropical Storm Lee, but this was on an entirely different scale, and the fear in this woman's voice was like nothing I'd heard. She was terrified. She felt doomed, forgotten, and enraged.

I walked toward her and collected my own emotions as best I could. "Ma'am, what's happening? What can we do?" I asked. "We can help you."

At first my words seemed to bounce off her. I kept repeating them, as I would have to Henry or Theo if one of them had woken from a nightmare, until she calmed down enough to explain: Her home was destroyed. For two nights she'd had no electricity, no running water, no food, and no clean clothes. Given that it was late October, the nights were getting colder. She believed she would not survive.

Other Staten Island residents joined our conversation. They needed food, water, clean clothes, and adequate shelter. They showed us their ravaged homes. Chuck and I reassured them that the Red Cross and other services were on the way, but that promise felt flimsy. These people needed basics, fast. What if the Red Cross trucks didn't get here quickly? What if the Red Cross didn't find these people on this block? The region was filled with suffering families. We had happened to walk down this street; there were many others like it.

I hugged the woman and told her that I'd make sure she got help. A staffer wrote down her address, called the Red Cross, and the dispatcher reported, again, that the trucks would arrive within a couple of hours. But a phone call? By a staffer? What good did that do? I felt like I was failing on so many levels. As a senator, I was intensely frustrated by our government's response. As an individual, I felt absurd in my warm fresh clothes, standing there talking, not doing anything concrete. I decided I needed to do something immediate and physical to help this woman. Yes, thousands of my constituents needed services, but this was the person standing in front of me. I could help her.

I asked one of my staff members, Andrew Borchini, a former attorney who'd just entered public service, to take my credit card and buy her food, clothing, and anything else she might need. So Andrew made his way back to lower Manhattan. The power was still out and almost everything was shut down, but he found an open Kmart on 34th Street and bought everything he imagined might be useful: underwear, socks, T-shirts, jeans, sweaters, jackets, scarves, food, water, and toilet paper.

The next day, Andrew went back to Staten Island and found the woman, who was then working with neighbors to haul mildewing couches and mattresses out of their homes. When Andrew handed her the bags, she started to cry. She thanked him for the clothes, water, and food, but she clung to the toilet paper. Such an inconsequential item, but at times the smallest gifts can feel like a very big deal.

We are all here to take care of one another. We all know this. Do unto others as you'd have them do unto you. It's better to give than to receive. These phrases are so timeworn they almost lose meaning. And yet they are well used for a reason: They are the cornerstone of life.

"If you can't feed a hundred, just feed one," Mother Teresa is often quoted as saying. I think about this when I'm feeling overwhelmed: far better to take a small action than to avoid a problem because it seems too big. The pot of soup for a sick friend, the visit to check on a widowed neighbor—these gestures make life feel meaningful and manageable. The world may be vast and slow to turn, but we will get where we need to go if we're kind and caring to one another, one small act at a time.

George Saunders, one of America's best contemporary-fiction writers, captured the importance of kindness in a commencement address he gave at Syracuse University in 2013. "What I regret most in my life are failures of kindness," he said. "Those moments when another human being was there, in front of me, suffering, and I responded . . . sensibly. Reservedly. Mildly." His advice for the young graduates was "Err in the direction of kindness. Do those things that incline you toward the big questions, and avoid the things that would reduce you and make you trivial. That luminous part of you that exists beyond personality—your soul, if you will—is as bright and shining as any that has ever been."

Hurricane Sandy hit just before Halloween. "Mommy, how will the kids go trick-or-treating?" Theo and Henry asked me with heartbreaking innocence, focusing on what they could understand. I told them that the storm was so bad that many kids probably wouldn't go trick-or-treating at all. So Henry and Theo were as kind as they knew how: They asked me to take those children some candy. The families in the homeless shelters throughout New York City were reeling. Chocolate was not the answer. But when I showed up at one in Manhattan with candy, along with books my boys had stopped reading, the adults were thankful to be cared for as individuals, even if in a tiny way, and the children, for a few hours, were giddy.

At that time, one of the biggest challenges public servants faced was figuring out how to channel all the aid pouring in to those who needed it. New York City was at its generous best, with relief tents and staging areas cropping up in every hard-hit community. Some collection sites were well organized; others, less so. In the Rockaways, in an open space across from the police station, clothing donations poured in so quickly that they began piling up. This would have been fine if the weather forecast was clear, but it called for more rain. We met with the community organizers, who were doing an amazing job but still didn't have enough manpower to rummage through the heaps, let alone deliver jackets and blankets to those who needed them most. We did not manage to move or tent the clothing before the showers began. Few in the area had working dryers, and nobody needed more wet clothes. I wish we could have done more.

Two days after that I visited a relief area on Coney Island, staged by FEMA with the help of the New York City Department of Health. This site, in the parking lot adjacent to the Brooklyn Cyclones baseball stadium, had tents, food, and communications equipment—but they, too, had hundreds of bags of unsorted donations. Meanwhile, lines of people waiting for coats, gloves, sweaters, blankets, food, and toiletries snaked out in all directions, and the queues kept stalling and growing longer, as the supply of jackets and blankets on hand for volunteers to dispense kept running low.

I walked over to the undifferentiated donation pile and started sorting, searching for coats and blankets. This wasn't much, but at least it was something. I convinced a few other people to join me and we all got to work, organizing piles of jackets and other warm items and delivering them to the volunteers to give away. Nobody deputized me to do this, and, to be honest, I'm not sure if it fit into the New York City health department's overall plan. But I hated standing around, useless. I hoped at least a few more families were warm that night.

For weeks after Sandy, I was depressed. I woke up every day with an empty feeling in the pit of my stomach, which stemmed from my inability to do nearly enough. Again and again, I'd tell Jonathan how awful and ineffective I felt, and he'd encourage me to hang in there. But I was breaking down—not eating right, skipping meals—and I could not keep my mind focused on anything positive. It kept drifting back to all the pain and devastation. In Westchester County, two boys were killed when a tree fell through the roof of a house. Twenty people in New York State drowned in their own homes. I couldn't fathom all the suffering; I felt unhinged even trying. Theoretically, at least, I held a position of power, yet I couldn't do anything of consequence. I dwelled on that for weeks.

Soon enough I realized that my energy was best spent fighting for money and resources for my constituents, so I began asking every senator I could for help. Senator Daniel Inouye, chairman of the Appropriations Committee, had seen many disasters in his time. He knew how useless I was feeling. "I know how devastating it is; I will help," he said, wise as always. I held on to his words. The bill to bring $60 billion of disaster aid to Sandy victims was the last Inouye ever wrote. Sadly, he died six weeks before it passed.

I also found purpose in testifying before my colleagues, telling the story of Glenda Moore and her two lost sons. I wanted to put a human face to the tragedy in a way that nobody had yet done. The morning of the testimony, I was so preoccupied that I just pulled my hair back in a clip and didn't bother to put on makeup. (I only wear makeup when I know I'll be photographed; the rest of the time, I'm barefaced.) So I looked exactly as wrung out as I felt when I told the Senate Committee on Environment and Public Works about Brendan and Connor Moore. Typically that committee hears testimony about infrastructure—not very emotional stuff. During my testimony I lost my composure and cried openly, and I didn't care. I was focused on what I'd learned from Mary Landrieu in my fights for the 9/11 healthcare bill and Don't Ask, Don't Tell. A two-year-old boy and a four-year-old boy had died. My objective was to tell the story of the pain and needs of people whose lives were devastated by the storm.

Thankfully, most of the time, life is less heart-wrenching, and a small measure of kindness can feel significant or at least boost somebody's day.

A couple of years ago, I watched a colleague fight like hell to win her reelection race. She was up against a self-funder who was spending a fortune on attack ads. The stress was causing her to lose so much weight so quickly that her suits sagged off her shoulders and hips. So I decided to buy her a little pick-me-up: a cute but professional pantsuit and matching blouse. (I've gotten pretty good at guessing sizes over the years.) One day, during votes, I led her into the private reception room off the Senate floor. "Just a present for your campaign," I said. "I know you don't have a minute for yourself."

She texted me right after she tried it on, thanking me and saying she was now ready to go out "and beat this guy!" She wore it to her next debate.

In my office, we help in more substantial and satisfying small ways. Most hours of most days, I'm not writing a new law or changing the world. I'm doing little tangible things—helping where I can by, say, making phone calls for people who are having trouble navigating the bureaucracy that stands between them and a green card or citizenship. My immigration team is so good at working the system. They know exactly whom to call, and when, and what needs to be said so the small important things happen, like somebody's grandmother attending a wedding or a child who is in the United States on a limited visa making it home for a family funeral.

Similarly, the small kindnesses people extend to me mean so much. I will never forget what Senator Dianne Feinstein did for me my first month in the Senate. She invited me to lunch and asked me if I might want some tips on managing my workload and keeping tabs on the hundreds of issues that crop up each week in a big state like New York. I said, "Yes, of course!" so she walked me through all the reports and updates she receives from her staff, explaining which ones she gets daily, which ones she gets weekly, how she keeps track of who's calling her office about what issues, where her legislation stands, and what her staff are working on. She even handed me her actual summary report—the weekly one—so I could study it in precise detail. This was a huge gift. She'd created her system through decades of trial, error, and careful consideration. I felt like I'd been handed the secret recipe for Coke or Pepsi! Dianne knew I was probably drowning in my new job. She offered me not just a rope, but a canoe with paddles.

The list of those who've helped me is long. One simple but life-changing example: A coach from Theo's baseball team—who's also the father of one of the players—regularly drives Theo home after practice. He must know that I feel awkward asking, because now he just offers, and his thoughtful gesture takes a huge weight off my mind. Theo's practice ends at 8:00 P.M., so if I pick him up myself,

Henry has to come in the car, and that keeps him up past his bed-time.

I try to pay it forward. In February 2012, a young woman named Tulsi Gabbard, who was running for Congress from the 2nd district of Hawaii, reached out to me. She'd entered the primary race six months earlier with little name recognition, and was still 45 percentage points behind the Democratic front-runner. But I believed in her. After 9/11 she'd volunteered to serve in Iraq. She then did a second tour in Kuwait, where her job was to train the all-male Kuwaiti National Guard. On her first day, many of the guardsmen refused to shake her hand or acknowledge her existence, but when they graduated, the men honored Tulsi with an award for her work. The day I met Tulsi I said to her, "We've got to get you to Congress so we can work together!" and I meant it, too. We need leaders like Tulsi, and I'd been where she was: a rookie nobody knew, far behind in my first race. I tapped into my network, reaching thousands of women and men dedicated to supporting good women candidates. And guess what? Tulsi won. She earned her own success, charging into a tough campaign and putting in all the hard work required to win. Tulsi is now the first Hindu member of Congress and the lead House sponsor of our bill to combat military sexual assault. (And she's a clutch player on our softball team!)

In my school community, I make a point of inviting two or three extra boys to the movies on a Saturday so their parents can go out on a date, or I walk a half dozen kids to their computer class when I walk Theo. At home, I try to make time for the details. Cooking Theo his favorite breaded chicken, finding the preferred soccer shorts again, playing Candy Land over and over, reading every Berenstain Bears book . . . Life happens in these small moments. They're often where the important lessons present themselves and the big truths emerge.

In my house, a significant part of the parenting job is listening to and decoding the myriad hurts, hopes, slights, and concerns Henry and Theo present me with each day. For instance, whenever Theo is complaining about feeling vaguely bad, I know he's not really sick. When he's sick, he's very specific. When his symptoms are amorphous, something happened at school. Often it'll take me more than twenty questions to dig out the root cause, because Theo is my reticent kid. But eventually he opens up and explains that he got in trouble for distracting a classmate when they both should have been listening, or a friend called him crazy when he was trying to be funny. Henry, on the other hand, is not shy. Far from it. His challenge is that he's all emotion. With him I have to wade through the soup of his feelings to find the solid issue underneath.

For example, just this morning Theo had a fever—a real one. He told me he was hot, and sure enough he was, so he had to stay home from school. Then Henry wanted to stay home, too, so he tried to fake sick.

First he said, "Mommy, I don't feel so good. I have a headache."

I said, "Well, try to go to school anyway and tough it out."

A minute later Henry said, "I feel like I have to throw up."

"If you throw up, I'll collect you from school and bring you to my office and you can throw up on Theo there."

Henry didn't get my joke, but he did finally come to his point. "I think you care more about Theo, because he gets to stay home!"

I'm sure you've been there: late, rushing to get out the door, when something profound comes into relief. I put down my bag, bent to Henry's level, and held him. "I love you very much," I said, "and we'll plan a 'Mommy and Henry' day soon. But sick days aren't fun. You'll have more fun at school than sitting in my office, doing nothing."

Henry glared at me; then he let it drop. Digging to the bottom of how someone feels is essential—at home, at work, everywhere. Henry did get his "Mommy and Henry" time later that week. While Theo was on a playdate, Henry and I spent the morning having brunch, getting his hair cut, buying him a new shirt for a special family dinner that night, and then he sat on my lap while I got a pedicure. I felt so blessed to have a day alone with him. Nothing consequential happened, and that's what made it perfect. My work life has plenty of drama. At home I try to focus on peace, love, and heart.

Chapter 10

My Real Inner Circle

One Sunday in December 2011, after waking up early, kissing my boys goodbye, catching a 9:44 A.M. flight from Reagan airport to Newark, speaking at a women's fundraiser in New Jersey, holding a press conference in midtown Manhattan, interviewing a candidate in my New York City office for a community-outreach position, and attending a lunch for State Senate Democrats, I escaped to my friend Angela's house on the Upper East Side.

I don't think I have ever been so happy to walk through a friend's door.

I knew in advance that the day was going to be long (and it was far from over—I still had a finance meeting and a fundraising dinner to attend). But I clung to the saving grace on my itinerary, a single line toward the bottom of the page: "2:30 P.M. to 4:30 P.M., Personal time."

"Personal time" on my schedule can mean many things: a doctor's appointment, a concert at school, a squash match. But that

Sunday it meant visiting Angela. The two of us had bonded over a thousand late nights during my years at Davis Polk.

The minute I walked into her apartment, I felt a wave of relief. You know what I'm talking about, that letting go that comes from the bone-deep comfort of being understood and unconditionally loved, knowing you can let your guard all the way down? I tossed my suit jacket, kicked off my shoes, and sat on a kitchen stool as Angela, five foot two with a smile that lights up a room, piled dishes in the sink from her children's late lunch. Her life is exactly as hectic as mine. She's now a partner at Davis Polk and she has two kids under five, which means she never has enough time to exercise, or be by herself or alone with her husband, or read a book for fun, or just exhale. But in spite of that—and because of it, too—we've always made time for our friendship. Friendship is the glue that holds me and all the parts of my life together.

We didn't talk about anything important that day—no cases, no elections, no sick parents, no pregnancies, no angst about our kids. Just the silly complaints we never get to share: how all that our British husbands want to do is go away for the weekend and race cars, how those husbands expect us to be parenting savants, how miserable grueling diets are. Angela had recently lost ten pounds, so she was down to a size four while I was back up to a six. I'd made a point of bringing a suitcase of suits and dresses for her to try on. Some of them I'd barely worn; others I shouldn't have bought in the first place. My girlfriends and I have always shared clothes. Angela pulled out for me some clothes that didn't fit her just then, including a red-and-black strapless Burberry dress that Jonathan had bought me pre-babies, which was now coming full-circle from my closet to Angela's closet back to mine. Sometimes a borrowed dress is exactly the boost you need.

Just as some men trade power tools, my girlfriends and I trade clothes. Since I started losing weight in 2010, I've borrowed tennis whites from my sister-in-law, Liz, and work clothes from my friend

Rachel. Even Rachel's sister gave me some hand-me-downs, which was a real gift, as she has fabulous taste and exactly the kind of elegant but serious outfits I need for work. Over the past five years, I've been every size from four to sixteen. Who can afford seven full wardrobes? I happily give away anything that I can't use. (When I was losing weight, I purposefully gave away my old smaller dresses. I liked the reward of buying new clothes when I dropped a size.) I even give my old work suits to my female staff. My general counsel, Michele Jawando, who's had three pregnancies, has made good use of whatever size fits her at the moment; the others take the rest. Jess often looks bewildered when he sees a junior staffer walking around in a blazer he's sure he's seen on me.

Before I left Angela's house that Sunday, I promised to send her a beaded dress that I bought when I was single but hadn't put on in years. We also made a plan for New Year's Eve so we could get together and wear our "new" elegant outfits. Then I was shot back out the door, into my finance meeting and my work dinner, the reality of my daily life.

Women talk a lot about juggling work and family, and it's a crucial conversation. But for me, the third leg of the stool, the one that keeps my life from toppling over, is friendship. It's a choice, not a responsibility. It's my respite from demands, the place I go to recharge myself so I have energy for all the rest: raising my children, nurturing my marriage, serving my constituents to the best of my ability, and caring for my extended family.

I travel a lot, but I have final control over my schedule, so I try to squeeze in visits with friends as often as I can. Sometimes it's just twenty minutes (and if I'm lucky, an hour or two) in Albany, Los Angeles, Denver, or London. Even a short check-in can keep me sane, especially when I'm feeling stretched too thin. My childhood friend Elaine once threw a birthday dinner party for me because I was too busy to plan anything and she knew I'd be depressed if December 9 rolled around and I was working yet again. Paige, who

I've known since high school, more than once invited my family over for Halloween because our house in Hudson was too rural for Theo and Henry to trick-or-treat door-to-door when they were very young. Caroline and Jennifer always find time for weekend summer barbecues.

My childhood friends have kept me centered more times than I can count. During my run for Congress in 2008, before my big debate with Sandy Treadwell, Elaine and Paige joined me back in the green room with snacks, because they know everything about me, including the fact that I get anxious, short-tempered, and unreasonable when I'm hungry. They joked with me about the absurd parts of the campaign to settle my nerves. Then they checked my teeth before I went onstage.

Being there for them means just as much. If one of my friends has a major life event, I do anything within my power to attend, even if it means planning my schedule six or nine months in advance. When my friend Alisandra asked me to be her daughter's godmother, I made sure I was in Los Angeles for the christening, just as I was sure to be in New York City for Lucy's daughters, in London for Gillian's son, and in Albany for all of Erin's kids. My girlfriends and I have held one another's hands through breakups and pre-wedding jitters, including hair and makeup crises that felt insurmountable at the time. We've absorbed all the bitching about swollen ankles and aching backs that come with pregnancies. And of course we've been there for one another in the hard moments, too. When Elaine needed someone to take care of her children for the day so she could move her mother, who was suffering with Alzheimer's, into an assisted-living facility, there was nowhere else I would have been.

Like too many working women with young families, I've had to rely on my children to help me make new friends in this phase of my life. I just don't have a spare second to meet new people and to build relationships from scratch. I've now spent two Valentine's Day dinners with Stephanie, a mom from Theo's school, the mother of his friend Wilson. (I must say Theo has excellent taste in friends.) Both our husbands travel a lot and were out of town, so the first Valentine's Day that we spent together with the boys, I cooked steak and vegetables, and we ladies shared a nice bottle of wine. The second, we planned to meet at La Loma, a local Mexican restaurant. That night turned into a bit of a fiasco, as La Loma has three locations (two related La Lomitas), and each of our families went to a different one, and my phone battery died from Henry playing too much Plants vs. Zombies. But we all met up, ordered lots of carne asada (no nachos—we were both on low-carb diets), and had a laugh.

Political friendships are different from personal ones, but they provide balance and warmth, as well. I say this in interviews a lot, but I think it bears repeating: One of the reasons why women in Congress have been so effective is that we actually know and like one another. In April 2009, my friend Debbie Wasserman Schultz organized a women's congressional softball team. The prior year, she'd been diagnosed with breast cancer. She didn't tell any of us on Capitol Hill about her illness until she'd recovered from her double mastectomy. But when she returned to work, she filled us in and asked if we would join a team to raise money for breast-cancer awareness among young women. I had never played softball. I didn't know the first thing about the game, and I was in terrible shape, still nursing Henry and having just started playing tennis again. But I jumped at the chance to play. Only one member of our team was under forty; the median age was well over fifty. We represented profoundly different districts. I was thrilled.

Our first practice took place in a small park for dog walkers, nicknamed "X Park" because the sidewalks cross in the middle. At that point, just swinging the bat and bending down to field a ball without pulling a muscle presented a major challenge for nearly all of us. But if there's one thing all members of Congress have in common, it's that we're competitive and willful. We wanted to win. So we practiced hard, learned the game, and took the field for our one matchup of the season with the gusto of Little Leaguers. I played shortstop and pitched a few innings and had one big hit. Our other pitcher was Grace Napolitano—age seventy-two and one of our ringers, because she'd played in high school. We were trounced by the young staffers from the Democratic and Republican National Committees, 15–8. But I was hooked.

I've played every season since, and over the past two I've started running early in the morning before practice with our coach, as well as Senator Kelly Ayotte and Congresswoman Shelley Moore Capito. They are all much faster than I am, but they're kind enough to slow down so we can chat about Shelley's son's wedding and Kelly's weekends with her kids. We all have distinct policy ideas and commitments to different causes, but none of that matters while running. Over three miles and an hour-long practice, we connect just as people. The first question I ask when a new female colleague joins the House or Senate is, "Do you want to play softball?" (I recruited Senator Heidi Heitkamp based on her campaign ads alone—she knocked several pitches out of the park.) The team binds us together in a way that is hard for many to fathom in political life.

The women in the Senate make time for one another off the field, as well. In 1988, Senator Barbara Mikulski initiated quarterly dinners. (At that point, the only attendees were Barbara and Nancy Kassebaum, from Kansas.) Her goal was to create a neutral space for female senators to talk and connect. The dinners have grown quite a bit since then, but we still uphold the three original rules: no staff, no leaks, no memos. It's amazing what a difference it makes to create a space in which we think of one another not as potential votes or allies but as daughters, wives, mothers, and friends. None of us thinks of each other as cooks—my female colleagues are some of the most accomplished and effective leaders in the world. But recently we've started taking turns hosting those dinners, and at risk of sounding like I'm trying to sell you a Junior League cookbook, Susan Collins makes an amazing sweet potato salad, Amy Klobuchar makes the best wild-rice salad I've ever eaten (she wins all sorts of Minnesota recipe contests), Claire McCaskill makes a delicious low-sugar berry cobbler, Lisa Murkowski cooks the salmon her husband catches in Alaska and stores in their freezer, and Barbara Mikulski knows exactly where to buy the best Maryland crab cakes.

We even once had a women's dinner in the Blue Room in the White House. One day I suggested to President Obama that he host a dinner; he said yes; and then, just as I had years earlier when Hillary asked me to host a fundraiser, I refused to let staffers back out of the idea and insisted we set a date. Lisa had been planning to host that quarter, so the White House chef served Alaskan halibut in her honor. That dinner was a little more formal than our usual get-togethers. We sat at a long table and President Obama listened as we each presented our ideas and raised issues. It was a great chance for the women in the Senate to amplify one another's voices. We are stronger when we can work together. More gets done.

I've also been lucky enough to form friendships with a few truly extraordinary women who have lived public lives. One is the actor Connie Britton. She and I went to college together, and the summer after my sophomore year we traveled to China. From the moment we stepped off the plane in Beijing, the experience was so overwhelming that a small group of us (Connie, myself, and two other friends, Amy and Dana) bonded. The coal dust in the air burned our eyes and left a film of soot on our skin by the end of each day. Our dorms were cement boxes with straw mats to sleep on, a hole in the floor for a toilet, and cold-water showers. The first night, at a ceremonial dinner, our hosts served a crispy whole fish, his big eyes staring up at us from the table like no Chinese food any of us had ever seen.

We fused as a group immediately, out of emotional need and a desire to help one another process what we were seeing—the poverty, the exotic (to us) culture. We also worked through the mundane stuff, too, like why it took my boyfriend so long to write. After about a month, Connie, Amy, Dana, and I found our bravery, taking trains to explore the country every weekend. We even geared up to lip-synch to Madonna at the American Embassy on the Fourth of July. Without one another, that trip would not have been nearly as rich. As a foursome, we were fearless—not that we realized it at the time.

After college, Connie and I lost track of each other. Years later, when she was back at Dartmouth for a reunion, another friend asked if she wanted to come hear me give a talk. Connie's reaction was: "Kirsten Gillibrand? Who the hell is that?" (She'd only ever known me as Tina Rutnik.) But we reconnected and have stayed in loose touch since. A few years ago, she called me when she was adopting her son, Eyob. Foreign adoptions can be slow and byzantine. Eyob needed treatment before he turned one year old, and the bureaucracy was churning so slowly that Connie worried he wouldn't get the care he needed in time. I told her I'd help in any way. I understood panic and urgency. Her son needed help. She was going to do everything possible for him.

Obviously, Connie's work is very different from mine (hers is far more glamorous). But it's been interesting to talk to her about the characters she's created, and there's a synergy in what we're both trying to do: make women's voices heard. In the movie version of *Friday Night Lights*, Connie played Tami Taylor, the football coach's wife. It was just an ornamental part, not exactly fulfilling, so when the executive producer, Peter Berg, asked Connie to play Tami Taylor again for the TV show, she hesitated. She'd grown tired of playing women who rarely spoke. After much begging on Peter's part, she agreed to the role—but with a serious caveat: Tami Taylor would have the strong voice of a strong woman. Connie would make sure of it.

As Connie tells the story, she was a bulldozer on the set, holding

Peter to his promise every step of the way. She did it in her graceful Southern way, but she was unstoppable, calling him every week when she got her script, pushing him to let her character go deeper. "I got into this thing and moved to Austin, Texas, and it was like, 'What the heck, and what was I thinking? Football and all these dudes?'" she told me recently. "But I knew it was time to step up and have the guts to find my voice. As a female actor, you bring your whole self to the job, and a big part of what you have to offer is your experience as a woman. You have to take risks. You have to go for it. If you wait to feel safe, if you stay on the sidelines, the big thing will never happen." Amen.

And then, of course, there's Gabby Giffords.

I felt bonded with Gabby even before we met, right after that first congressional election when I saw her on TV. We met that fall in Washington, and she's the closest thing I have had to a sister in Congress. We started at the same time, both of us in our mid-thirties (I'm a few years older), both from historically Republican districts. We grew together and pushed each other to build normal and intimate lives, which is not easy to do in Washington. Just after New Year's in 2011, Jonathan and I and Gabby and her husband, Mark Kelly, double-dated at Matchbox on 8th Street on Capitol Hill; it's their favorite spot. Gabby and I talked about tough campaigns and complained about harsh opponents. Gabby and Mark told us about their recent trip to Rome, where they'd attended midnight mass at the Vatican and spent countless hours enjoying the art and architecture.

A week later, on January 8, while Gabby was holding a Congress on Your Corner event at a Safeway near Tucson, Arizona, she and eighteen others were shot, six killed.

When Congressman Heath Shuler, a mutual friend, called to tell me the news, I was standing in a model home, looking at tiles and finishes. Jonathan saw my face crumple from across the room. We left immediately and started driving toward home. Halfway there, we stopped at a restaurant because I didn't want Theo and Henry, who were home with a sitter, to see me so upset. While we sat at the restaurant's bar, Debbie Wasserman Schultz called. She was in Florida, driving her seven-year-old to a soccer tournament. She said she'd heard that Gabby's shot was fatal.

"We just don't know that yet. We don't know for sure," I said, refusing to believe it was true and making Debbie promise that we'd both keep scanning reports until the facts became clear.

For what felt like an hour, I sat there in shock, shaking and crying. Jonathan wrapped his arm around me to try to calm me down. The world felt like it had telescoped to just the two of us and our thoughts and prayers about Gabby. Jonathan kept refreshing the news reports on his iPhone, and we finally learned that the reports of Gabby's death were false. I called Debbie immediately—she was still driving. Then Jonathan and I drove home, hoping we could keep it together in front of the kids.

For days, cable news reported on the shooting around the clock, interviewing any member of Congress they could get in front of a camera, many of whom didn't know Gabby at all. One colleague called her "perky," which would have annoyed her for sure. I wanted to be left alone in a dark room to worry and grieve. Six people had died. My communications team had been getting dozens of requests for me to do interviews and had been turning down all of them. But when Pia Carusone, Gabby's chief of staff, contacted Jess to ask if I would please speak about Gabby on TV, I felt I had to say yes. Shining a light on her true character was one thing I could do for her in such a horrible time of need.

Four days later, on January 12, when I was trying to pick myself up and return to doing the work that Gabby and I shared, I received an invitation to join President Obama for a trip to Arizona. He also invited Debbie, Nancy Pelosi, and the whole Arizona delegation for a day of remembrance to honor the victims of the shooting. I raced home to change and was on Air Force One within three hours. I was so grateful to the president for including me. Tragedy makes a person feel powerless and alone. That invitation helped ease my sense of isolation.

That day in Arizona was one of the most emotional of my life. Just after we touched down in Tucson, Speaker Pelosi, Debbie, and I all visited Gabby in the hospital. Mark had warned us that Gabby's face was expressionless and her eyes were closed. Seeing her was not easy—bandages all over her head, a tube coming out of her mouth.

I stood at her side and held her hand. She'd been my partner in public service since before we met. I didn't know how much hope was reasonable to have. She was so strong and surrounded by so much love, but her injuries were so grave. But as Debbie and I stood there, talking about the future we prayed we would have together, we saw Gabby struggle to open her one unbandaged eye. Mark grabbed her hand, leaned in toward her, and said, "Gabby, can you see me?" The room became silent and still.

"Gabby, can you see?" Mark said. "Show me a sign!"

Slowly, she lifted her right hand a few inches off the bed and struggled to raise her thumb. We all started to sob. In that moment, Gabby showed Mark and the rest of us that she was with us 100 percent and understood what we were saying. I stood there in awe of her will and determination in the face of evil.

The president's speech later that afternoon was so powerful. He honored all those who had been murdered: Judge John Roll, who'd dropped by the Safeway to say hello to Gabby on his way home from church; Phyllis Schneck, who had three children, seven grandchildren, and a two-year-old great-granddaughter; Dorothy Morris, whose husband, George Morris, was shot while trying to save Dorothy's life; Gabe Zimmerman, Gabby's outreach director, who was engaged to be married the following year; Dorwan Stoddard, who also took a bullet for his wife, and was killed; and nine-year-old Christina-Taylor Green, the only girl on her Little League team. She'd been born on September 11, 2001, and she planned to be the first woman to play Major League baseball.

"Imagine—imagine for a moment, here was a young girl who was just becoming aware of our democracy, just beginning to understand the obligations of citizenship, just starting to glimpse the fact that someday she, too, might play a part in shaping her nation's future," President Obama said, calling on all of us to honor Christina's life. "She had been elected to her student council. She saw public service as something exciting and hopeful. She was off to meet her congresswoman, someone she was sure was good and important and might be a role model. She saw all this through the eyes of a child, undimmed by the cynicism or vitriol that we adults all too often just take for granted.

"I want to live up to her expectations. I want our democracy to be as good as Christina imagined it. I want America to be as good as she imagined it. All of us—we should do everything we can to make sure this country lives up to our children's expectations."

Over the next year, I continued to visit Gabby in various hospitals and at home. One night, I slept in her hospital room so I could be there when she woke at 6:00 A.M. Each time I saw Gabby, her positive spirit and progress amazed me. In January 2012, just a year after the shooting, Gabby flew back to D.C. to attend the president's State of the Union address. Before the event, we did a little shopping at Forecast, my favorite clothing store on Capitol Hill. Gabby still had a gift certificate from the store that she'd received as a wedding gift. That day we both tried on a few things, and Gabby chose a bright-red top that looked beautiful on her. For a moment I felt like nothing had changed, that we were back to being freshman congresswomen, our lives on a shared course. But of course everything had changed. Gabby had survived such a dark passage. She battled her way through a year of speech and physical therapy, fed by her own spirit and her husband's love. She had shown the country what resilience looks like.

That evening, when she walked onto the House floor for President Obama's State of the Union address, the nation's eyes were on her. Our friends are our foils and our confidants, the people we seek out to make us feel whole in a way that sometimes not even family can. When Gabby waved to the nation, unbowed, I felt so proud to call her my friend. She radiated a triumph of sorts, a refusal to surrender to hate. I felt so moved. I knew she'd be back, fighting to make life better for all Americans, and she is.

Chapter 11

A Time Such as This

Sometimes in life you get a sense of meaning and mission from chasing your dreams; other times, the meaning and mission find you. A problem surfaces, a need appears, and whether you intended it or not, you happen to be the right person in the right place and at the right time to lead the fight. Undoubtedly, you had other plans: a soccer team you wanted to coach, a used-book drive you wanted to start, or a half marathon you wanted to train for. But it's important to stop and listen when something of real consequence inserts itself into your life, tugs on your conscience, and won't let go.

That's how I began my battle against the Department of Defense on how the military handles sexual assault within its ranks. I had not planned to take on this issue. To be honest, for my first four years as a public servant, I had no idea how bad it was. But then I started hearing stories of men and women who'd suffered the worst things imaginable while serving our country. Compounding the problem, commanders failed to prosecute the perpetrators of terrible crimes.

These men and women needed a voice. They needed a champion with a megaphone, and I happened to have one. Fighting for them has become one of the most important things I've done in my career.

Full disclosure: I had to be asked twice to learn about the problem before I adopted it as a cause. In 2012, a good friend who was working on a documentary about sexual assault in the military asked me to take some time to understand the issue. I said, "Of course I will!" But I said it in the same casual spirit that I say, "Of course I will!" to a lot of requests. What I meant was, I'll keep an eye open, and when a bill or hearing comes along, I'll pay attention and report back. That year, during our debate of the annual defense bill (where the Armed Services Committee works on the military's budget for the year), the issue arose in the context of women not wanting to have to disclose a rape in order to have access to healthcare and abortion services while serving abroad as well as the fact that there were convicted rapists still serving in the military. Senator Jeanne Shaheen and I worked on and passed amendments to fix both, but we had only scratched the surface of the problem.

Then another friend, Maria Cuomo Cole, called my attention to the issue. She was one of the executive producers of that same documentary, called *The Invisible War*. Directed by Kirby Dick and produced by Amy Ziering, it was now finished, and Maria asked me to take a look at the issue again. I said, "Of course I will," but this time with a little more commitment. I figured that spending ninety minutes watching the film would help me broaden my understanding of an issue. I cared about the military, particularly the military personnel. Yet I certainly didn't imagine that their struggles would define mine.

I scheduled a viewing of *The Invisible War* with my senior staff. When the hour arrived, Brooke Jamison, my legislative director; Anne Bradley, my deputy chief of staff; Bethany Lesser, my D.C. communications director; three women on my military staff—Elana Broitman, Brook Gesser, and Katie Parker—and several other women in my office all showed up punctually in the conference room. Who was missing? Both the men.

"There's no way we're watching this without the guys here. This is ridiculous," I said, walking out to find Jess and Glen. When I found them at their desks, on their cellphones, I explained to them that this was not an invitation; it was a requirement. So they shuffled into the conference room with me, and we all watched together in horrible stillness as a string of service men and women told stories of being raped by their peers and superiors and how afterward the military had disregarded them or blamed them for the crimes.

Nothing in my life—not sitting on the Armed Services Committee, not even the anguish of watching 9/11 first responders dying from diseases caused by their work at Ground Zero—prepared me for what I saw in that film. These men and women were violated in the worst possible ways by their own brothers and sisters in uniform, then they were betrayed again by our military leaders. Crimes could be reported to anyone, but all power rested with the commanders, as the commanders had sole authority to decide whether to prosecute a case or not. Commanders even had the authority to throw out a jury verdict after a perpetrator was convicted. These commanders had no legal training or objectivity, but they did have many possible biases. They had asses to cover, reputations to maintain, favored service members to protect. Military justice for sexual-assault survivors was a farce. I knew that I had to fight for men and women like Stacey Thompson. A sergeant spiked her drink, raped her, and left her on the street at 4:00 A.M. When she reported the attack, the sergeant's friends retaliated against her, telling investigators that Stacey used drugs. The investigators then called her a liar and reassigned her and eventually kicked her out of the military with an other-than-honorable discharge. Brian Lewis was a twenty-year-old fire technician on the USS *Frank Cable,* a submarine tender out of Guam. He wanted to have a long naval career, so when a superior officer offered to give him some advice over dinner, Brian said yes. After dinner, the officer raped Brian. Brian was ordered by a commander not to report the crime. Instead, he was forced to go back out to sea with his rapist. Trina McDonald, a navy veteran from Kentucky, served on a remote base in Alaska, the only woman among ten men. She was brutalized and raped repeatedly by military police and men in her chain of command; at one point she was thrown into the Bering Sea.

Whatever it took, I had to help bring justice to these survivors, and I needed to work to prevent future crimes. I told my staff to start making a plan to fight for change. Top priority: Get survivors' stories heard.

The next week, in a stroke of excellent timing, I was offered the opportunity to choose a subcommittee chairmanship. The Personnel Subcommittee on the Armed Services Committee was still available, and I jumped at it. I knew exactly what I was going to do first: hold a hearing on military sexual assault and ask the victims to testify. All Americans, but especially those of us in government, needed to understand the problem, however upsetting the stories might be. We needed to recognize that we were allowing a climate to exist in which many thousands of service men and women are raped each year, and then we are turning our backs on them.

The scale and depth of the problem were unthinkable. When I first started advocating on this issue, the latest Department of Defense report on sexual assault was from 2011, and it indicated that an estimated nineteen thousand men and women in uniform were subject to rape, sexual assault, and unwanted sexual contact each year. Of that huge number, only about one in ten cases was reported. Half of the female victims who filled out the Department of Defense survey said that they didn't report the crime because they feared their commanders would do nothing with their case, and almost half said they did not report because they feared or witnessed retaliation. Even if a victim summoned the courage to report a sexual assault, the chances of justice were slim, as only one in ten of the reported cases resulted in conviction, partly because each commander, despite the lack of legal training, had the authority to toss out a case before it went to trial. What if the commander was involved in the crime? What if he wanted to protect the accused because they were friends? He could just declare the case closed. Of the one percent of sexual-assault cases that made it all the way to a conviction, only three-quarters of that one percent led to a perpetrator serving time, as at the very end of the process the commander still had absolute power. He could say, "This jury verdict doesn't seem right to me," and toss the sentence out.

In March 2013, at the first hearing I held as chair of the Personnel Subcommittee, I did my best to get out of the way and let the survivors speak. I even slotted the survivors to speak at the beginning so the military brass would have to hear them. (Normally the commanders testify first, then leave.) One brave woman, Rebekah Havrilla, told Senators Carl Levin, Lindsey Graham, Barbara Boxer, and the others assembled that for the first year and a half after she was raped, she didn't tell anybody—it didn't seem worth it, because she had such a slim chance of receiving justice and such a high one of being retaliated against. Then she found out that the man who raped her had posted online some explicit pictures of her being violated. That made reporting it seem worth it, whatever the cost, so she brought the crime to the attention of the Army Criminal Investigation Command (commonly known as CID). As she hoped, a formal investigation commenced. This involved Havrilla spending four hours with a male CID agent going over in minute detail the explicit pictures of her being raped. After that meeting, Havrilla did not hear from the CID for four months. Then an investigator called and asked her to come back and go over the pictures again. She did. Six months after that, the case was closed.

Also at that hearing, BriGette McCoy testified that she was raped on her first assignment in the military when she was just eighteen. Later that year, she was raped again by another soldier. A third soldier who repeatedly harassed her repositioned McCoy to work with him in a locked, windowless space. McCoy, traumatized and terrified, wrote a formal complaint, which the commander never pursued. Instead, she was threatened with prosecution under the Uniform Code of Military Justice, and so she chose to leave the military instead of facing judgment for a crime committed against her. When she returned home, she was so depressed and unstable she tried to commit suicide.

Unbelievably, in that hearing, Lieutenant General Richard Harding and Major General Vaughn Ary both tried to defend the status quo, saying it was essential to maintaining "good order and discipline" to keep all legal decisions within the chain of command, including the decision to overturn a jury verdict. This made me furious. By what accounting were nineteen thousand sexual assaults a year good order and discipline?! I was irate—and I could also see that I had a long, hard battle ahead. Day one, and the good ol' boys were closing ranks.

My team got right to work on legislation to take the decision to prosecute sexual assault out of the military's chain of command. This is what the victims said they needed. I didn't believe this was the radical reform that its opponents argued it was. Many of our allies had taken decision-making on whether to prosecute serious crimes out of the chain of command, and their commanders' abilities to control, train, and deploy effective troops had not suffered. Israel made the change in 1955; England, Canada, Australia, Netherlands, and Germany all changed during the last decade. All of their militaries were stronger because of the reform.

Adding fuel to my fury, within a few weeks the Department of Defense issued a new report, estimating twenty-six thousand cases of military sexual assault in 2012, up seven thousand from 2011.

Worse, the percentage of people willing to report crimes perpe-
trated against them had gone down. At our next hearing, in May
2013, when the generals again tried to argue that commanders
needed the authority to decide which crimes to prosecute in order to
maintain good order and discipline, I did my best to contain my
rage. How could nineteen thousand or twenty-six thousand sexual
assaults a year represent anything other than a total breakdown of
discipline and accountability? Did the generals even understand
what sexual assault meant?

Thankfully, along with my anger, my legal training kicked in.

"Now, General Welsh," I found myself saying, "you said you
didn't know what we'd be fixing by removing the authority from
the chain of command. . . . Do you have a sense as to why, if there
are nineteen thousand or twenty-six thousand or some unknown
number of sexual assaults and rapes within the military every year,
why such a fraction are reported?"

Back in my law days, I'd done a lot of depositions. In them, my
job was to ask probing questions. If someone gave a vague or im-
plausible answer, I then kept asking one question after another,
hammering for clarity until I got to the truth.

"Could you surmise that it may well be that a victim has no faith
in the chain of command on this issue, on sexual assault?

"Do you think, perhaps, that a victim does not believe he or she
will receive justice because the chain of command is not trained,
does not have the understanding of what sexual assault and rape
actually is?

"Imagine you are the assaulted victim who has just gone through
a trial. And because a commanding officer has said, 'Let's overturn
the jury's verdict,' you then have to salute the person who assaulted
you."

I really lost my patience that day—I was furious. Afterward, I
worried that I was too aggressive and might have appeared un-

hinged. My staff tried to reassure me. Yes, that was intense, maybe right near the line, but it was effective. I hoped to God they were right.

The Senate Armed Services Committee met again in June to further discuss the problem of sexual assault in the military and how we might create more accountability and justice. This time, when the generals sat before me in a row and started saying that same ridiculous line, that we needed to keep decision-making about whether to prosecute sexual assault in the chain of command for the sake of "good order and discipline," I lost it, for real.

On the surface I was calm and collected. But I'd had it with their bullshit and their condescension. My voice started to rise as my argument started to form. "You have lost the trust of the men and women who rely on you, that you will actually bring justice in these cases," I said. "They're afraid to report. They think their careers will be over. They fear retaliation. They fear being blamed. That is our biggest challenge right there." My argument was growing with urgency. An expert on nonverbal communication later analyzed my rate of speech and my body language, calling out a bunch of gestures that I never even knew had names: pseudo-prayer hand-chop, conventional steeple. He declared that my out-of-body experience up on the panel behind the microphone must have been authentic. "Not all commanders are objective," I continued, gathering strength and momentum with each point. "Not every single commander necessarily wants women on the force. Not every single commander believes what a sexual assault is. Not every single commander can distinguish between a slap on the ass and a rape, because they merge all of these crimes together."

People often remark that it's hard for women to get angry in public and still be taken seriously. On that day, and on many days after it, I didn't care. These generals were protecting the status quo and their power, not the most important asset our country has: the men and women who serve it. One of the victims who had come forward to tell the story of her rape looked like a sixteen-year-old girl. She entered the armed services a virgin, and after everything she suffered in the attack, she hated to have to call her dad and tell him why she wasn't a virgin anymore. Still the commanders sat at that table, defending the system that looked the other way from tens of thousands of sexual assaults each year. That was how little they valued the men and women who suffered among their ranks. Adding to their cruel failure to protect their people, the military undermined the survivors' credibility. If a woman was raped, it was her own fault. She'd been drinking, maybe, or she'd walked back to the barracks alone at night.

Over the next few months, through the summer of 2013, the issue was regularly in the national headlines, and I started to meet with my fellow senators one by one, seeking their support for legislation to take prosecuting sexual assault in the military out of the chain of command. Some of my peers had experience with the issue. (For example, Senator Richard Blumenthal was a former attorney general and was on board from day one; Senators Boxer, Collins, and Mikulski had long histories of fighting these battles.) Others didn't. When I spoke to newcomers, I'd ask them to think like a father, a brother, or a husband, someone who feels a duty to care for others.

Most Democrats quickly understood the need for reform. And about half the time, Republicans did, too. But the other half of the time, I'd find myself talking to someone who was taking the Department of Defense's position at face value and not delving any deeper. I started every meeting with the basic facts and then listened to questions and concerns, taking care to be patient, forthcoming, and frank. I think it helped to be a woman, with a lot of experience talking about personal topics. Comfort with verbalizing an issue is a real asset when trying to steer a colleague toward compassion.

I've worked relentlessly to bring every senator who would hear me out over to our side. So much so that after approaching Senator Bob Corker, an old-school conservative from Tennessee, on the Senate floor a couple of times, he started our first meeting in his office by saying, "I don't want you to take this the wrong way, Kirsten, but you're what my family would call a honey badger." I went back to my office and watched the hilarious YouTube clip about this crazed creature that will stop at nothing to get its prey. I decided to take it as a compliment.

The fight was exhausting. On days when I met with survivors, I felt motivated to push on and press until justice was done. But unsuccessful meetings with other politicians and procedural hurdles took their toll. Through the summer and fall of 2013, I spoke regularly with Senator Carl Levin, the longtime chairman of the Armed Services Committee, someone whose insights I value. He'd been a key ally in repealing Don't Ask, Don't Tell, so I knew he was willing to take on the Department of Defense. But I felt my heart sink one day when we were discussing the distinction between allowing commanders to decide when to prosecute and giving them the ability to overturn a jury verdict. In my mind, commanders shouldn't have either right, since both allow for bias and untrained decision-making, which we would never allow anywhere else in society. But when Carl said to me, "I see the issue differently," my hope of having his support was lost.

Still, we made progress. Defense Secretary Chuck Hagel agreed that no commanders should overturn a jury verdict. The Department of Defense itself agreed that that authority is a vestige of pre–World War I military law. Numerous commanders have been caught behaving badly, which of course undermines the argument that commanders should have this sole authority. And while they didn't go far enough, some really good reforms were passed by Congress.

The support from across the aisle was tremendous, too. Senator Susan Collins, who has always been a strong voice for victims' rights and is not afraid to take on the status quo, liked our idea of reform from the start. Senator Lisa Murkowski also wanted to help, though her motivation was more personal and her commitment more emotional. Earlier in her career, she'd recommended a young woman to a service academy and, once there, the young woman was raped and did not receive justice. Lisa became determined to make the military safe for other young women like her. A few senators with libertarian streaks have also rallied to our side. One day, Senator Chuck Grassley, who is well respected among Republicans for his years of service and his willingness to take on powerful interests, walked up to me on the Senate floor and said, "I read about your bill, Kirsten, and I think what you're doing is important. Count me in!" Senator Rand Paul supported us, too, and, perhaps most unlikely, so did Senator Ted Cruz. Cruz is a former Supreme Court lawyer, and after listening to my argument in a committee hearing, he announced right there that he agreed with my position. Afterward, he spoke on our behalf at his caucus meetings to make our case to his undecided colleagues. The New York *Daily News* was so shocked by his support that they ran the headline WHEN HELL FROZE OVER!

More than occasionally, I've thought that if more women served in Congress, this issue would have been a no-brainer (seventeen of the twenty female senators supported our reform) and so much time and energy would not have been burned on this fight. Recently, *The Buffalo News* ran a political cartoon of me approaching a general, again, with a caption of the general saying, "Ever hear the expression, 'No means no'?" But I believe we're getting there, one step at a time. One hearing that gave me hope was the Defense Advisory Committee on Women in the Services. I had the privilege to testify and made the most impassioned plea I could muster, telling the personal stories of service men and women who were raped and then disregarded or retaliated against when they tried to report the crimes. The panel voted ten in favor of reform, six abstaining, none against. That vote didn't move Senator Levin, Secretary Hagel, or

President Obama. But I know in my heart we will win their support someday, and when we do, they will cite that Defense Advisory Committee on Women in the Services vote.

The first setback we suffered happened just before Thanksgiving in 2013. A vote was finally scheduled, with a full day of debate on the Senate floor. Senator after senator made arguments for and against. My allies spoke strongly and eloquently. Momentum and urgency were on our side. Then the Republicans decided to obstruct Senate business. Democrats had just enacted limited filibuster reform (a totally separate issue), so Republican leadership decided to respond by objecting to all amendments, including ours, and that canceled our vote. It was a blow to the advocates, the survivors, and to me. We picked ourselves up and kept fighting, but we'd been ready for the vote that day.

The vote finally came in March 2014. For procedural reasons, we knew we'd need sixty votes to overcome a filibuster, and by then fifty-five senators had declared their support. At least a half dozen more were undecided, including Mitch McConnell, the Republican leader, and Mike Enzi, who'd supported me on the 9/11 healthcare bill and who I believed was on our side again. Marco Rubio, Thad Cochran, and Tom Coburn had also expressed grave concerns about the status quo, but we didn't know how they'd swing. That morning I met with both Mike Enzi and Chuck Grassley, to further brief the issue for Mike. Another senator who had co-sponsored the bill asked for an emergency meeting—never a good sign. After a half hour of dissecting the fine points of the bill, he let me know he could not vote with us. I was crushed.

Down on the Senate floor, the debate began. Our stalwarts— Senators Barbara Boxer, Jeanne Shaheen, Mazie Hirono, Chuck Grassley, Dean Heller, and Rand Paul—all made impassioned pleas. Richard Blumenthal and Ted Cruz would have spoken, too, if we had more time. I closed the debate with my best two minutes, telling survivors' stories and expressing in their own words why the system was broken and needed this reform. Then they called the vote. We lost two supporters and we gained two. That left us with fifty-five votes for reform—five short. I was devastated.

I looked over to the group of senators standing together to my left in the back of the chamber, all people I count as close friends. I was afraid to hug Senator Heidi Heitkamp, because I thought I'd start to cry. But I managed to hold it together and embraced her, Joe Donnelly, and Amy Klobuchar, and then I started to shake the hands of supporters and opponents alike. Many said, "You couldn't have done more!" or "Next time." I was grateful for their goodwill, but I was wrecked—physically and emotionally depleted.

Moments after the vote, I texted Jonathan to tell him what happened and to check on Henry, who was home sick with a fever. Jonathan had taken an earlier train than usual back from New York to provide moral support. He wrote back immediately: "Well done, bunny—sorry about the people you work with." He was waiting to catch me as I collapsed when I walked through the door, dinner already made and on the table.

Days like that, when I feel most defeated, I start to question whether I should be a senator at all. When I can, I try to shift my focus from work and onto small, doable things: reading my children stories, getting them to bed by eight o'clock, turning in by eight-thirty myself and reading a few pages before I turn out the light. This battle bores deep into my soul. There's so much suffering, so much failing, the worst of human nature on display. I wish I could say that I can pull myself out of these depressions with a phone chat with my sister, Erin, or a great squash game. But I can't. It's not that easy. The injustice is too devastating. The rate of suicide and PTSD among sexual-assault survivors is too high.

But walking away from the fight is not an option. Not fighting means the greatest failure of all. When morale among my staff sinks and they feel sure we're going to lose, I tell them the same thing: We will keep fighting, without question, because fighting is the right thing. Men and women are getting brutally raped, and military leaders aren't doing enough to change it—we cannot sit idly by. Other people on Capitol Hill might think we're crazy for taking on a losing battle and not letting go, but so what? There is no question about our commitment. We will fight to the end.

During my very darkest moments, when not even cuddling Henry and Theo can make a day feel a little brighter, I look to my faith. Raised a Catholic, I've always enjoyed attending church, and I look back very fondly on the period in my twenties and thirties when I was involved in my Bible study class. Each week, we would read a passage and write down answers to a few questions about it. Then we'd come together in a church around 60th and Park, not far from my office, to share our interpretations and ideas. That study group was the antidote I needed to an uninspiring job at a corporate law firm (suffice it to say, it wasn't God's work). I'm so thankful for those years of study now. Whenever my life feels out of my control or when I question whether I've chosen the right way, faith offers me deeper meaning and guideposts.

Lately I've been thinking a lot about the story of Esther. For those who don't know that story—and at risk of oversimplifying for those who do—Esther was a young woman chosen by King Ahasuerus to replace his first wife, from whom he'd become estranged. Esther was Jewish, but the king didn't know that. Nor did the king know that one of his advisors was corrupt and planned to kill all the Jews.

Esther's uncle learned of the advisor's plan and pleaded with her to intervene. This was no small request. If Esther approached the king without being summoned, she risked being executed. If she didn't approach the king and the advisor carried out his plan, her people would die. The uncle did his best to persuade Esther to act, to use her unique position for the greater good. Perhaps a higher force had put her in that place at that time for this reason, Esther's uncle told her (Esther 4:14, New International Version): "For if you remain silent at this time, relief and deliverance for the Jews will arise from another place, but you and your father's family will perish. And who knows but that you have come to your royal position for a time such as this?"

Those last six words—"for a time such as this"—resonate with me to my core. I believe that in certain situations, we each have a moral responsibility to act. We all have unique opportunities that derive from our unique circumstances, and we have a duty to take them. Esther, of course, rose to the occasion. Smart woman that she was, she orchestrated a way for the king to learn the plans of his evil advisor and save the Jews.

Rewriting the law on sexual assault in the military is my unique opportunity. It demands that I use all of my powers: my legal background, my seat in the Senate, my empathy, my tenacity. We've had setbacks, but I've kept going. You know that old saying "When God closes a door, he opens a window"? That phrase is as important to me as "for a time such as this." It's so true. Just when I'm positive we've hit an insurmountable roadblock, we find a new source of strength. I just got off the phone with a survivor to thank her for her advocacy. Her words of humility, gratitude, and fearlessness reminded me again why I am here.

In battling the status quo, I'm constantly inspired by my friend Gabby. Most of us think of her and curse the darkness. So much cruelty in the attack against her, so much loss in its wake. For the first year after the shooting, that was my focus, too. I dwelled on Gabby's losses: her speech, her ability to move her right side, her capacity to serve in Congress. I dwelled on the death of nine-year-old Christina-Taylor Green, who had gone to see her favorite congresswoman that day. Today I spend more time in awe of what

Gabby has gained: the strength to take on what might be the toughest status quo of all in our country, America's zero-sum view on guns. Gabby has such confidence and conviction now. She knows she was put here "for a time such as this," that this is the battle she was meant to fight. Her husband, Mark Kelly, the decorated astronaut, looks at her with so much love and respect. They are on a mission, working together to build a network to support gun reform, and they're fully aware of the unique position they're in. They are the right people at the right time. They know they can save lives.

What do you do when an issue finds you? First of all, don't feel like you have to attack it on your own. Regardless of what you're fighting for—speed bumps on your block, more-nutritious lunches in schools—know that you will find allies. These allies may not be obvious from the start. Often you won't see who they are until you're out on the field. The same is true for seeing the best course of action. You can't always visualize the path to victory from the sidelines, but once you're in the game, it becomes clearer and clearer with every twist and turn. And, second, remember that the most worthwhile achievements in life never come easy. With every setback, you gain strength, resolve, a tougher skin, and new insights.

This fight has taken everything I have and given so much back to me, too. It's shown women the importance of getting involved in politics. It gives me a powerful sense of purpose every day. Along the way, I've found moral support everywhere. My general counsel, Michele, shares my love of inspirational Scripture and sends me readings by email when she knows I'm struggling. My chief of staff, Jess, always says, "Armor of God!" when I'm nervous or intimidated before a big meeting—it's both a serious piece of Scripture and our personal, funny war cry. My colleague Senator Barbara Boxer is always there when I need a boost, too. Just the other day when I was feeling demoralized, she said, "Kirsten, don't give up now. You have to keep fighting. These men and women need you and our efforts." She put me right back on track.

Naturally, I turn to Jonathan, too. He encourages me when I'm hopeless and absorbs the emotional brunt of hearing stories about some of the worst in humanity day after day. But it's often the strangers in uniform who buoy me the most. Last year, at the White House congressional Christmas party, a young woman in a naval uniform who was staffing the event approached Jonathan and me and said, "Senator Gillibrand, I can't tell you my name, but I wanted to tell you how much I appreciate your advocacy for us service members. It's making a difference." She had tears in her eyes, and a moment later, Jonathan and I did, too.

"Bunny, you have to keep fighting," he said to me. "Don't ever give up."

Chapter 12

Get in the Game

When Henry was in daycare, I'd often walk into his classroom at the end of the day and find him playing trains with his friends. Just one of those plastic Fisher-Price sets, with the station and the bridge and the round little humans. One day I found him in his usual spot, the train up on the table, playing with a girl named Sadie. He was moving the train on the track, reporting where it was going. She was moving the people, explaining where the men, women, and children were headed and what they'd do when they got to their destinations.

I asked Henry to please collect his coat and backpack. We still needed to pick up Theo from tae kwon do, and I wanted to get home and make dinner before it got too late. But later that night, after dinner and baths, my mind drifted back to Sadie and Henry playing with the train at school and where their dreams might lead them from there. I knew that when he grew up, Henry planned to become either the mayor of D.C. (so he could fix the roads near our house) or a train engineer. Those childhood aspirations made sense. Jonathan is an engineer, as is Jonathan's father, so neither a career in politics nor one in engineering seemed all that far-fetched. But I started wondering if Sadie dreamed of being an engineer, too—if her creativity and imagination would take her from playing on the table in daycare, thinking about the individuals and their relationships to one another, into a future where she worked to make sure that the trains took people where they needed to be, so they could do what they wanted to do with their lives. More than anything, I didn't want her to see her role as ancillary, her interests relegated to the side of the tracks. I wanted her to see herself and her pursuit as central and her point of view as necessary. I wanted her to take her questions and interests—"Where do people need to go? And with whom?" "What will their experiences be like?"—and run with them. I wanted her to grow from a girl playing Fisher-Price trains with Henry into a powerhouse of urban planning.

"Because we're women." I think about that phrase all the time. There's so much in it. So much talent, so much potential. And yet we still have so far to go before women's ideas, voices, and concerns are heard as loudly and clearly as men's.

I was lucky enough to have strong women inspire me at important moments, starting with my mother and grandmother in childhood, my squash coach, Aggie, in college, and Hillary Clinton when I was a young lawyer looking to make more of my life. We all have windows in time when we are especially impressionable, when the right words or actions can cause us to pivot in meaningful ways. A girl in Henry's prekindergarten class, Irina, has a father who does science experiments with her at home. And guess what she wants to be when she grows up? A scientist. Even at age five she dreams of building and creating something beyond herself, of having a career that will impact the world.

Irina and all the girls who dream big give me great hope for the future. Each of us, at all stages of our lives, needs to be open to inspiration. Just as important, all of us, as a collective, need to encourage each other's dreams. We need to aim high and stretch our shared vision of what seems possible. We need to believe in each other's best selves. We've made lots of progress in creating a just and equal world, but we have a ways to go. We need to make sure that girls like Irina are not exceptions because eight out of nine of the fastest-growing industries require proficiency in the so-called STEM fields (science, technology, engineering, and math). We need to guarantee that some of our children don't drift away from the tracks while others charge ahead, steering the train.

You matter. Your frame of reference is a strength. When women contribute and rise to positions of power, we bring our unique experiences and priorities with us, and we make the world a better, richer place. Beth Mooney is a perfect example. She started her career as a bank secretary, earning $10,000 a year. Now she's the chairman and CEO of KeyCorp—and the first woman among the top-twenty bank chiefs in America—and she runs her company differently from others because of who she is. In 2005, she supported her Key colleague Maria Coyne in starting a program called Key4Women to support female entrepreneurs. Women often have a harder time securing capital than men do, in part because few banks and venture-capital firms are managed by women. Over the years, Mooney and Coyne have lent over $6 billion to women-run businesses. Would a pair of men have made the same effort? I doubt it. Similarly, Denise Nappier—the first African American woman elected to the office of state treasurer in the United States, and the first female treasurer in Connecticut history—has dedicated herself to ensuring that women and minorities serve on the boards of directors of corporations in which she invests the state's pension funds.

You don't need to wait until you control a bank to start making a difference. Among entrepreneurs, women who follow their passions can galvanize others to do the same. In 1989, Missy Parks, a former Yale University tennis, basketball, and lacrosse player, took her love of sports and her desire to find athletic gear that really worked for her and started the women's sports-apparel company Title Nine. The first year was far from great. She sent out thirty-thousand catalogs and received only fifty-six orders. But she persevered, never losing faith in herself or her mission, and Title Nine has grown 15 percent year after year since. She now carries pretty much everything a female athlete might need (including about a hundred different sports bras). Title Nine has also launched the Starting Block, a not-for-profit program that gives grant money to grassroots organizations committed to getting girls "off the sidelines and onto the fields." This is especially meaningful to me, as, according to a recent study, the single greatest predictor of whether a woman will run for public office someday is whether she played competitive sports as a kid.

Supporting women is not just good for women. It's good for everybody. When you look at the economy as a whole, the companies with the greatest number of women on their boards outperform the companies with the fewest. The number of women on a board correlates positively with social responsibility and reputation. The more women, the better the corporate governance.

Right now, it's not easy for women, particularly women with young children, to get where they need to go in their professional lives. Yes, women are trying hard to raise themselves up economically, and, yes, they're earning more college and advanced degrees than men. But our society doesn't support them. Daycare is too expensive; pre-K is not guaranteed; family leave is a pipe dream; the minimum wage is too low; and still women do not earn equal pay when compared to men. Leadership at companies big and small in America is largely male, and it shows. A recent study from Harvard Business School found that executives, both male and female, see the Gordian knot of combining work and family as a woman's problem, not a problem for everyone.

We can't sit around and wait for other people to solve those issues. We must work to solve them ourselves. I often think back to what Geraldine Ferraro said in her 1984 convention speech, when she was the Democratic nominee for vice president: "It's not what America can do for women, it's what women can do for America." At the time that she said those words, I had just graduated from high school and I didn't really get it. But I do now. Women have so much talent, intelligence, and expertise—we need to make sure America gains everything we have to give.

We can start by demanding that we have a broader public conversation, one that's not just about having it all or not having it all, or leaning in or leaning out, but one that includes a plan for lifting women up off the sticky floor. For that, we need structural change. We need new and better policies that support women and allow all women to rise. We need to end the cycle of women studying hard, starting careers, climbing through the ranks, taking time off to care for children, and never again finding a job as good as the one they left. We need to end the cycle of women working to support their families, getting a toehold on the American dream, and then losing their jobs and financial security when their children become sick, because they have no paid family leave. Women represent 62 percent of minimum-wage workers, whose earning power, adjusted for inflation, is at an historic low. Families with children under five years old spend more than 10 percent of their household budgets on childcare. Women continue to earn just seventy-seven cents on the dollar for what men earn, and even less for Latina and African American women. How can women and their families get ahead when they're getting undercut and shortchanged?

We need to use the power we have as women to shape a country that supports all of us. We need to vote for elected officials who understand all of our issues. We need to hold our representatives accountable once we've elected them. I hate to say this, but we've let the women's movement slip away. In 2010, under a Democratic pro-choice president and with a Democratic pro-choice female speaker of the House, we allowed the Stupak-Pitts Amendment to come to a vote. That amendment sought to deny women the right to purchase healthcare and reproductive services *with their own money*. What happened after Stupak-Pitts passed in the House of Representatives? Nothing. Zilch. Women did not rise up, consolidate our power, and come down on the cowards with force. Congress betrayed half the population, and no one paid a price.

There are women doing amazing things, and you should be one of them. Debbie Sterling, who graduated with a degree in mechanical engineering and product design from Stanford, started Goldie-Blox, a toy company aimed at inspiring girls to become engineers. Her product line touched such a nerve that GoldieBlox beat out fifteen thousand other small companies in a contest to have their ad aired during the Super Bowl. The GoldieBlox spot showed girls blasting old pink dollhouses and toy kitchen appliances into space.

Or take Edie Windsor. She sued the United States government to recognize the validity of her marriage to another woman, and at age eighty-four, she saw the Supreme Court rule in her favor, striking down the Defense of Marriage Act's federal prohibition on recognizing same-sex marriage. Edie's willingness to speak out, use her story, and fight caused a major shift in the United States and healed a personal pain in so many individuals' lives. State by state, our country is overcoming decades of injustice and allowing people to marry the ones they love, whatever gender those people might be. And we have Edie, a fiery octogenarian, to thank.

Others are just starting the fight. Just recently, I walked into my office before a press conference about sexual assault on college campuses, and two young women greeted me. Both attended an Ivy League school and both had been through hell: first surviving violent assaults, then suffering the trauma of reporting those assaults to incompetent campus review panels that belittled them. At the press conference, I watched one of the young women train her eyes on the cameras and relive the worse moments of her life. Her delivery was flawless; her courage strengthened with every word. She possessed more power at that moment than any board member or college president. Just by telling her story, speaking truth to authority, she was changing the world.

We have unimaginable strength. This college senior never imagined she'd be raped, and she never imagined the university would turn its back on her. But she refused to let those events define or defeat her. She claimed the power of her voice and used her story and her pain to make life better for others.

We all need to do this: speak up, gather strength, support one another. If we do, women will sit at every table of power, making decisions. In Hollywood we'll have more films and television shows that depict women as intelligent, courageous, principled leaders, not as T and A. In business, we'll have more products and services that meet our needs. In communities, we'll have safer streets, cleaner air, and greater sustainability. In our homes, we'll have less domestic violence and child abuse. In government, we'll have policies that allow all Americans to thrive and reflect what we believe.

How can you become part of this change? The first step is to think about giving. This starts, for all of us, at home. I believe it's essential to instill in our children a feeling of gratitude for what they have and a desire to help others with less. Every year my boys and I go through all their clothes, toys, and books and decide what they should donate to other children who need those items more. These lessons are reinforced at the boys' school, where each Christmas, we collect hats and gloves and hang them on a giving tree and buy gifts from Santa for a boy in our community who might otherwise go without. One year the boys helped organize a book drive to serve those most in need in our community. Each Wednesday all the children bring in extra food to share with local families who don't have enough.

How can you get off the sidelines in your own life? Here are just a few ideas to think about. Start with yourself: Wake up thirty minutes earlier in the morning and go for a walk or jog so you can face the day from a stronger, healthier, happier place. Practice compassion with yourself and others. In your community, volunteer to feed families in need at your church. Visit someone who is lonely. Plant trees or a community garden to teach your kids about sustainability. At work, sponsor a talented young woman. Donate business clothes you no longer wear to Dress for Success, a great organization that gives clothes and other professional-development assistance to women who need a boost jump-starting their careers. At home, snuggle up next to your daughter and learn to how to program through the zombie games on code.org. Give your niece a mini-microscope for her birthday. Teach your boys that girls are smart and valuable, even if they find them curious. Above all, protect your children's most daring childhood dreams.

Inside the political process, blog, tweet, or write letters to the editor holding elected officials accountable. Drive senior citizens to the polls. Make sure your friends and family vote. If you really want to step it up, organize a fundraiser or write a check to your favorite candidate—even $10 can make a difference. Best yet, run for elected office. I promise you, representing your fellow citizens is more fun, more fulfilling, and less scary than it seems. If you end up here in Washington, I promise to take it upon myself to keep you off the sidelines. I probably have a suit in your size, and we could really use another starting pitcher for the women's congressional softball team.

ACKNOWLEDGMENTS

With much gratitude, I'd like to thank all the people who helped make writing this book possible. Top among them: my editor, Jennie Tung; my collaborator, Elizabeth Weil; my lawyer, Bob Barnett; and all the wonderful people at Ballantine Books. A special thanks to Secretary Hillary Clinton for writing such a kind foreword and being such an invaluable role model, mentor, and friend.

I'd also like to thank my staff for their endless patience and years of excellent public service.

With much love, I'm grateful to my dear friends and family, my wonderful husband, Jonathan, and my greatest blessings, Theo and Henry, for keeping me happy and centered on what's most important.

Most deeply, I'd like to thank all the women who have inspired me by speaking out and making their voices heard. This book is for you.

RESOURCES

General (All Women)

American Association of University Women
www.aauw.org

Catalyst
www.catalyst.org

Dress For Success
www.dressforsuccess.org

Higher Heights for America
www.higherheightsforamerica.org

League of Women Voters
www.lwv.org

Makers
www.makers.com

National Organization for Women
now.org

National Partnership for Women & Families
www.nationalpartnership.org

National Women's Law Center
www.nwlc.org

The Shriver Report
shriverreport.org

Young Women and Girls

The Girl Effect
www.girleffect.org

Girl Scouts
www.girlscouts.org

GEMS (Girls Educational & Mentoring Services)
www.gems-girls.org

Girls Inc.
www.girlsinc.org

Girls Who Code
girlswhocode.com

Ignite (Inspiring Girls Now in Technology Evolution)
www.igniteworldwide.org

Million Women Mentors
www.millionwomenmentors.org

International Women

Equality Now
www.equalitynow.org

Every Mother Counts
everymothercounts.org

Half the Sky Movement
www.halftheskymovement.org

The Malala Fund
malalafund.org

UN Women
www.unwomen.org

Vital Voices Global Partnership
www.vitalvoices.org

Women for Women International
www.womenforwomen.org

Women in the World Foundation
www.thedailybeast.com/witw.html

Running for Office

Center for American Women and Politics
www.cawp.rutgers.edu

The Eleanor Roosevelt Legacy
www.eleanorslegacy.com

Elect Her—Campus Women Win
www.aauw.org/what-we-do/campus-programs/
elect-her-campus-women-win

Emerge America
www.emergeamerica.org

EMILY's List
www.emilyslist.org

Run Women Run
www.runwomenrun.org

Running Start
runningstartonline.org

She Should Run
www.sheshouldrun.org

Women's Campaign Fund
www.wcfonline.org

The Women's Campaign School at Yale University
www.wcsyale.org

Building a Community

BlogHer
www.blogher.com

Lean In
leanin.org

Levo League
www.levo.com

Moms Rising
www.momsrising.org

UltraViolet
www.weareultraviolet.org